# Beyond Meetings

Lessons and Successes in Advising Student
Organizations

# BEYOND MEETINGS

## LESSONS AND SUCCESSES
### IN ADVISING STUDENT ORGANIZATIONS

COLLABORATIVELY CREATED BY

DR. CINDY KANE & BECCA FICK
· SERIES EDITORS ·

SUE CAULFIELD
· ILLUSTRATOR ·

TOM KRIEGLSTEIN & ALEX FIELDS
· BOOK EDITORS ·

# Beyond Meetings

## Lessons and Successes in Advising Student Organizations

### Collaboratively Created By

Dr. Cindy Kane – Series Editor

Becca Fick – Series Editor

Sue Caulfield – Illustrator

Alex Fields – Book Editor

Tom Krieglstein – Book Editor

# Other Student Affairs Collective Books

*Men in Student Affairs*

*From the Beginning: Perspectives from New and Emerging SA Pros*

*Hello My Name Is Committed: Stories About Dealing with Mental Illness in Student Affairs*

All titles can be viewed and ordered at
www.StudentAffairsCollective.org/Bookstore

A Student Affairs Collective Book - Volume 4

Beyond Meetings: Lessons and Successes in Advising Student Organizations

Printed in the United States of America

Design by Student Affairs Collective

10 9 8 7 6 5 4 3

Student Affairs Collective
www.StudentAffairsCollective.org
info@studentaffairscollective.org
Phone: (877) 479-4385
Fax: (206) 337-0259

## >> Contact for bulk order discounts <<

## About The Student Affairs Collective

As with all great ideas, the Student Affairs Collective (www.StudentAffairsCollective.org) began as a series of doodles on the back of a napkin by Tom Krieglstein & Kevin Prentiss in 2005. The vision was, and still is, to create the ultimate online community of Student Affairs Professionals in which everyone is both a teacher and student at the same time to help each other play, learn and grow together to collectively reach higher levels of success.

In the beginning, Tom and Kevin wrote all the content. They then bribed their Student Affairs friends with cookies and digital unicorns to help them write more content, and slowly, over time, an engaged community developed. The SA Collective started to become the go-to place online for Student Affairs professionals to receive and share knowledge from their peers. The growth remained steady, and then Twitter came along...

In 2009, over lunch with Debra Sanborn at an Iowa coffee shop, Tom pitched the idea of a weekly chat via Twitter for Student Affairs professionals. Debra nodded excitedly at the idea (as she does with all new ideas), and a couple weeks later, on Oct 8th, 2009, the first #SAChat happened with 15 people and 50 tweets.

Since then, the SAC, which is what the cool kids call it, has grown to be a community of thousands of Student Affairs professionals, stretching international borders and all functional areas of the field. We now have a podcast, a book club, a jobs board, a member directory with learning communities, a weekly newsletter, Tweetups, and the #SAChat Awards. Through it all, the SAC continues to focus on creating the best online, low cost, peer-to-peer learning network for Student Affairs professionals.

Now it's your turn to jump in and be a part of the family and help us create the next ten years of awesomeness. As a bonus, you'll laugh, smile, create friendships, and grow a positive national reputation for yourself and your work. Then, when you go on to change the world, we'll get to say you first shared your potential with us by helping fellow Student Affairs Professionals be even more amazing!

# How To Use This Book

While this entire book in focused around one main theme, each individual author takes on a unique perspective around the main theme. Some chapters might be totally relevant to your current situation and others not so much. Reading this book from beginning to end is probably not going to be as valuable as looking at the Table of Contents and skipping ahead to the chapters that are most relevant to your current situation.

# Share The Love Online

We love seeing when fellow Student Affairs Professionals take their professional development into their own hands. If you take a photo of you with this book and share it online via one of the channels listed below, we'll send you a special little gift in return!

On Twitter post your photo using one of these two methods:
> Use the #SAChat hashtag
> Tag the @The_SA_Blog account

On Facebook post your photo to one of these two groups:
> Student Affairs Professionals >
https://www.facebook.com/groups/2204795643/

Student Affairs Collective >
https://www.facebook.com/SACollective

## To the contributors

This book is possible because of your commitment to sharing the experiences of student organization advising and your belief in the impact that is possible through supporting students in this way. We hope that sharing your story has been another great step in the journey to share the positive contributions you are making to student learning each and every day.

## To the students

If we had all of your student organization advisors in one room, they would all want to thank you for the part you play in their success as advisors, so we will do it for them. Student organization advising is truly a teaching and learning journey for all involved and we know we speak for each of the contributors when we thank you for what you teach us every day.

## To the collaborators

Thank you to Tom and the Student Affairs Collective for your support of this idea and your belief in the value of sharing these stories with the broader community. The chance to bring these stories together in a collective voice is a wonderful opportunity to advance the profession and you all have made that possible.

- Cindy & Becca

# table of contents

# introduction.

Introduction - Dr. Cindy Kane

What would the average person say if you stopped anyone on the sidewalks of your campus and asked that person, "Where can I find an advisor?"

I'm quite confident that the first response would be to answer on behalf of the academic advisor. The next step would probably be to the career advisor, depending on the terminology used on your campus. However, the identity of the student organization advisor may not always make the immediate list. We could talk for a while about why that is, but my first thought is that it happens because the work of the student organization advisor takes place largely after 5:00 p.m., on weekends, and sometimes during the "free time" that a generous person contributes toward supporting students.

I rarely hear the student organization advisor role discussed outside of our own circles, but the potential for this connection between advisors and students is vast. In my recent research, I had the wonderful opportunity to hear from campus activities professionals about their regard for the advising role as intimately connected to the teaching and learning process on campus. One participant said,

*I think [advising programming board] is my favorite teaching opportunity. I associate teaching with making a connection. Maybe I'm not giving them specific philosophy or theory or practices, but I'm learning about them. Through learning about them, I can teach them different perspectives, and I can teach myself a lot at the same time.*

The National Academic Advising Association takes this message of "Advising as Teaching" and explores it thoroughly in this great resource. Our professional associations in campus activities DO support dialogue about advising practices in venues like professional conferences, but the role of "advisor" is not just taken on by the campus activities professional. It's the biology faculty member who advises the Biology Club, it's the Resident Director who advises the Residence Hall Association, and the Assistant Director of Alumni Relations who advises the Senior Class Committee too. These folks are working daily with students and play a key role in the student learning experience.

Is student organization advising a teaching role? Is it a risk management/in loco parentis role? Is it both? How do we know? The answer can't only be "bring all of those people to a conference" or "have the activities office develop an advisor program." The challenges are deeper than that, especially given that the dialogue about the student organization advisor role is largely disconnected from other advising activities on campus and may not be reaching as large an audience as it could in the discussion of student learning.

This book was designed with a goal of widening the conversation about advising student organizations. This book contains wisdom from a range of professionals who have contributed their thoughts on the role of the student organization advisor on the college campus.

*"Our hopes in creating this book are to share their stories of successes and challenges in the student organization advising role, in the name of opening conversation about how to maximize the educational impact of this role."*

**Our hopes in creating this book are to share their stories of successes and challenges in the student organization advising role, in the name of opening conversation about how to maximize the educational impact of this role.** While we love the idea that student organization advisors will get this book, we love the idea even more that we share this book with others in the university environment.

Think about it – who else on campus might enjoy a peek into the experiences of these talented educators? Share this book with a colleague and we will then expand our collective knowledge one step further.

Happy reading!

*Cindy has served in a leadership role for the Office of Student Involvement and Leadership at Bridgewater State University since September of 1998. She is a consultant, speaker and program reviewer for associations and colleges and has served in leadership roles with the National Association for Campus Activities. In her time outside of work, she is a proud parent of her favorite emerging leader, @littleredsaid and is considering forwarding her phone calls and mail to the town Little League fields for the duration of the summer.*

# other duties as assumed

Other Duties As Assumed – Becca Fick

I love the spring carnivals, orientations, karaoke nights, and field trips to local sporting events. These are the things I share on social media and what friends and family think I do all day. And it's true, these are definitely a part of my job as a Student Affairs professional, but it's not the whole picture. And truthfully? **It's only part of why I come to work every day. I'm also here for the Other Duties As Assumed.**

Lest you confuse these tasks with "Other Duties As Assigned," let me show you the difference. No one asks us to do these things. We're not evaluated on them and our merit increases aren't attached to their success. We take on these tasks, above and beyond our regular job descriptions and committee assignments. **We do it because we find value in it, not because we're compensated or praised.**

Sometimes it's writing recommendation letters, meeting their parents during Homecoming Weekend, attending their thesis defense, and cheering them on at their games. But sometimes it's not all free t-shirts and balloon arches. Sometimes it's hard.

The days when a student can't pay her tuition bill because she has to help pay her family's back rent. Or when he's falling behind in classes because he's also working part time, and his newest sibling was up crying all night, and he's navigating his 3rd funeral of the year. (Real funerals – not the kind that suddenly pop up when a paper is late).

> "We do it because we find value in it, not because we're compensated or praised."

When she looks at you with tears brimming and explains that she's...late. Or when he loses his athletic scholarship and RA position because of a bonehead Thursday night (or a series of them).

When you spend hours supporting and encouraging them through these situations and it's still not enough. They drop out. They assure you they'll be back next semester, that they'll enroll in community college classes until they can save up some money or raise their GPA.

**When you realize that you are the first adult that has looked them in the eyes and told them that you're proud of them. Or that you're not.**

That you know they aren't meeting the expectations you've set. That you care enough to hold them accountable, even when it's hard and it hurts. You're not a social worker or counselor, but you may be the first person they've trusted, let their guard down for, wanted to impress – or at least not disappoint.

These are the other duties as assumed. **These are the things that sometimes come before emails, between meetings, and occasionally in late night text messages and phone calls.** There are no CAS standards for this. But sometimes, without these most basic needs being met, nothing else stands a chance of succeeding or mattering.

Oh, but when they do succeed? There is nothing sweeter! Watching students cross the stage at graduation is the ultimate reward. The path isn't always straight, but they've reached the finish line. **No matter how many times we ask families to hold their applause until the end, I revel in the whooping and hollering that explodes when these students hold their diplomas.**

 *Becca Fick is a writer, educator, and speaker. As an educator, her role is to help college students learn about themselves and the difference they want to make in the world. She enjoys reading, yoga, and running and fuels her adventures with coffee, craft beer, and wine. Becca also blogs at beccafick.com and can be found on Twitter @Becca_Fick.*

# BEYOND BELONGING:
## Leadership Development for Multicultural Organizations

Beyond Belonging: Leadership Development for Multicultural Organizations – Tricia Brand

Without truly understanding it, I began my journey with advising student organizations in 1994, when I co-led two groups at my Washington University in St. Louis campus. One was a new Campus Y organization devoted to anti-racism work with students in public schools; the other organization, the Women's Center, was well-known for student led initiatives that examined and confronted sexism, homophobia and violence present on our campus. My experiences as a student leader taught me so much about myself and even more about what it meant to represent a cause, a resource, and a visible (often marginalized) identity on a college campus. As a student of color at a predominantly white institution (PWI), I engaged on campus based upon my interests, but also in the way I thought others perceived me—as a Black, socially and politically conscious woman. I did not run for student government, I didn't become a Resident Advisor, I didn't join a campus activities board or the student newspaper—I didn't see these so-called "mainstream" activities as spaces where I belonged.

Years later, I became a Student Affairs professional, supporting student organizations whose missions were to create safe spaces and a sense of belonging for underrepresented students at PWI's. I intentionally reflected on my experiences as a college student, as I observed student leaders repeating the same behaviors that my contemporaries and I practiced. My student advisees typically became involved with one organization (where strong social ties and campus resources were present), and often graduated from college feeling that they weren't fully supported by campus leaders and students who did not identify with them racially, ethnically, or culturally. Some advisors of multicultural organizations describe this as the "diversity bubble." This is where students feel a great sense of belonging and influence in designated spaces, but experience limited cross-cultural dialogue and interaction, and develop limited interest or opportunities to assume leadership in "mainstream" organizations—such as student government, new student orientation, and residential life. This is not about preference, but a matter of emotional survival. On many campuses, the historical legacy of exclusion continues to shape the experiences of underrepresented students (Harper & Hurtado, 2007) and student interactions are profoundly and negatively impacted as a result. Feeling validated in social environments is critical to student involvement and leadership development—particularly among students of color at PWI's.

Pursuant to the resonant question Beverly Tatum explored in her book, *Why Are All The Black Kids Sitting Together in the Cafeteria?*, administrators often ask why so few students of color get involved with the more "traditional" leadership opportunities. Advisors who support student leaders in multicultural organizations and cultural centers must regularly educate colleagues about the "cultural incongruence" many students of color perceive with mainstream activities (Griffin, et al, 2008). However, there is an obligation we all have to mitigate this incongruence. With every new group of students, we have an opportunity to develop transformational leadership experiences within affinity-based spaces that foster intentional pathways to incorporate underrepresented students into mainstream leadership opportunities—where their voices and ideas are also essential.

Leadership learning and development occur through interactions within communities of shared identity, as well as across communities of difference (Dugan, et al., 2012). Described below are five approaches that are intended to help organization advisors of multicultural organizations develop and foster leadership identity at PWI's.

1. **Design activities aimed at helping student organizational leaders better navigate the university system.** There is a complexity to the college environment that very few students understand and optimize. Underrepresented student leaders especially require road maps to systems where they have been historically marginalized or excluded.

2. **Design leadership initiatives that develop mastery in highly transferable professional competencies,** such as budgeting, event planning, marketing, program evaluation, grant writing, and fundraising. Work with student leaders to create a competency map which presents skills they should practice and master by the time they complete their leadership role within their organization. Establishing confidence and proficiency in transferable skills validates students in a learning environment outside the classroom, and is more easily applied in other contexts.

3. **Establish opportunities that support students collaborating with other organizations.** One essential way to increase cross-cultural engagement and increase diverse programming within more "mainstream" organizations is to encourage and incentivize collaboration among other student organizations. The benefits that emerge from this approach to organizational planning are numerous, and often lead to broader student involvement on campus.

4. **Develop the capacity to identify, resist and respond to racism and microaggressions.** Often, culturally or affinity-based clubs and organizations have an unspoken "dual

mission" of supporting underrepresented students and responding to racially-charged incidents on campus that intimidate and invalidate students of color. Research indicates that internalization of negative stereotypes affects academic performance, educational motivation, and social self-efficacy for students of color (Steele, 1997). Student leaders require tools to respond to racism and microaggressions at PWI's, and a safe space to practice those tools in a peer-led environment.

5. **Apply inclusive leadership models for training and student development, with an emphasis on students self-defining.** The Social Change Model (SCM) of leadership development is a great example, as it promotes values of equity, inclusion, citizenship and service. This model highlights student empowerment and is intended to establish strategies for positive social change. This offers great value to students of color, offering meaningful ways to map their leadership journey in the context of addressing issues identified in their campus environment.

 *Tricia D. Brand is Associate Dean of Student Development at Portland Community College. Her professional and personal commitments are to diversity, equity and achievement in higher education and dedicates her time to leading a variety of programs and academic services for first-generation, low-income, and historically underrepresented students. She would like to hear from you, find her on Twitter: @triciabrand*

# SETTING BOUNDARIES WHEN ADVISING AS A GRADUATE STUDENT

But You're Just Like Me...Setting Boundaries When Advising as a Graduate Student - Ashley Jones

Let me set the stage for my journey as a graduate student advisor: In 2011, I graduated from Youngstown State University (go Penguins!) with my degree in Special Education. After a year and a half teaching, learning and a great deal of self-awareness and resilience, my journey ultimately led me back to YSU in the Counseling, Student Affairs Leadership and Practice program in the summer of 2013. During my undergraduate years, I was an active member of our local sorority, Alpha Omega Pi (later recolonized to become Alpha Omicron Pi). I was elated to participate in the alumnae initiate process with Alpha Omicron Pi and officially joined the organization in October 2013.

As a new graduate student, I knew that I wanted to experience student organization advising. What better way to do so than to advise for the organization that had given so much to me? I was far enough removed, right? With the exception of the current Chapter President, the majority of the active collegiate members had not been in chapter with me. The only other prior relationship I had was with the Chapter Advisor, the same person who advised when I was serving as President. It was the perfect setting. **Yet I quickly found that no matter how perfect the setting, advising student organizations requires one thing over all: boundaries.**

I was advising our VP of Academic Development. We had gotten off to a great start. I felt that I was appropriately coaching and mentoring not only the young woman who was my direct advisee, but our Academic Development committee at large. Our first handbook revision had gone splendidly, everyone was on board and ready to implement new academic programming initiatives.

No more than two days later, the tear-filled phone calls and text messages began coming in, including screen shots of members who did not agree with the new initiatives. **My issue wasn't that this communication was taking place, but that more often than not, the text messages would come throughout the work day with follow-up texts when a response wasn't received immediately.** The phone calls would easily last 1-2 hours and generally began around 9 PM. I found myself driving over to the collegiate member's residence hall after a grueling night of graduate classes to discuss how she should go about handling the most recent academic situation.

**A month passed and it felt that every free moment I had was being spent advising in some way.** I found myself sitting with a member of my graduate school cohort, who was also a YSU alum and a member of our Greek community during her undergraduate years. As I was venting, she said something that stuck with me: "It's because they think you're just like them". That was when it hit me. **The women I was advising saw me as her peer.** I was taking classes in the same buildings she was. My partner had been a member of the Greek community at YSU, very similar to many of the women. Not to mention, I lived on campus. I was not nearly as far removed as I thought. I was so eager to advise that I had never taken the opportunity to discuss my role and expectations with the women I was advising.

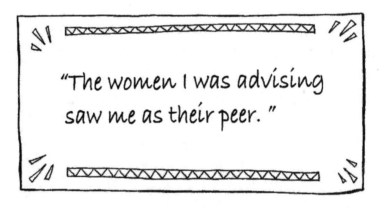

"The women I was advising saw me as their peer."

Even after this epiphany, I knew that I was not going to be able to establish strict boundaries with my advisee mid-way through the semester because that was not fair to her. **However, come fall semester, I sat down with my advisee and we had a great discussion about appropriate boundaries within our advisor-advisee relationship.** Let me tell you, it made a world of difference! I now very rarely feel as though I am burning the candle at both ends. Advising has quickly taken a turn from being something that I felt I had to do to improve as a professional, to something that I genuinely enjoy doing.

My suggestions for boundaries are these: it all depends what you are most comfortable with, and the way in which you prefer communicating. Here is what worked for me:

1.  **Conflict Resolution Strategies** – My advisee and I spent a great deal of time discussing conflict resolution strategies and how she would be able to implement them. This made moments that were formerly recognized as emergencies seem not so overwhelming to her. She felt much more confident handling the situation on her own without engaging me in every step of the process. This informally assisted in setting boundaries because it dramatically decreased the late-night, panicked text messages.

2.  **Scheduled Communication Times** – We set up a weekly communication time (Friday at 12 PM to be exact) where my advisee knew that she would update me and be able to ask questions. She knew that for that hour, she had my undivided attention.

3. **Meetings should not happen after 8 PM** – Plain and simple, no one should have to be in a meeting after 8 PM. I believe it is an important professional skill for advisees to be respectful of their own, their advisor, and their committee's time. Yes, 8 PM may seem like the best time because everyone watches Scandal together at 9, but when you are a professional you are going to have to schedule meetings during business hours. This is good practice.

Advising an organization so near and dear to my heart has been one of my most rewarding experiences I have had as a graduate student. I hope my story can help others in setting boundaries with their student organizations and enjoying their time as an organization advisor!

*Ashley Jones, Youngstown State University. I am currently completing my second year in the Counseling, Student Affairs Leadership & Practice Program at Youngstown State University. I serve as the Residential Education Graduate Assistant for our Office of Housing & Residence Life and am completing my internship in our Student Activities Office. My passion is inspiring and engaging students in all of their curricular and co-curricular opportunities. Twitter Handle: @Ashley__Jones01*

## Changing Your Default – Michael Giacalone

Student: "What do we do about this?" Silence. And suddenly all eyes are on me. Uh oh...at that moment I knew I had to change the way I was advising the organization.

Advising student organizations is more of an art than a science. I often think of advising organizations as a balance between giving support and providing direction. **An organization needs support so students become both owners and creators of their organization, but they also need direction to learn how to navigate unknown processes or policies.** In my mind, a "good" balance is one where the organization generally runs themselves, but the advisor is there to assist with tasks. For instance, an advisor can help interpret campus policies or steer members away from proverbial "cliffs."

As I tell my faculty and staff advisors all the time, "advising is going to change from organization to organization and from semester to semester." Change is necessary based on a variety of factors, including the experience and personalities of current leaders, experience of membership, and the campus culture. I would imagine, however, that we all have a default level of providing support and direction with student organizations which we are comfortable with and revert to in new or stressful advising situations. **Therefore, to adjust the way one advises requires both an awareness of the current method of advising and a willingness to change.**

The above scenario occurred during my second semester as an advisor to the Sorority Council. The Sorority Council was a two year-old group in the process of transitioning into a chartered College Panhellenic Council (which essentially means that we were adjusting to a number of new rules and processes). Reflecting back on that semester, I can now see that I was providing them with too much direction. **I was new to the institution and they knew I was familiar with both the Panhellenic requirements and the process of forming a governing council, so they looked to me as the "expert," which resulted in them taking my advice with little to no questioning.**

Quite honestly, I liked the way things were running. It was my first time as a fraternity and sorority life professional, I had knowledge and experience to impart on to the members, **and I felt like I had something to prove** – to my students, to my supervisor, and to my institution, which valued fraternity and sorority life enough to hire a full-time person to work with them.

Until that moment, **I didn't realize I was being much more directive than supportive, which was hard for me to accept.** This situation made me think about my own default level of advising. I value student autonomy, organization self-governance, and group decision-making without too much of my influence, but maybe my default level is too directive to fully live these values. Clearly, in that "all eyes on me" moment I was not working within that set of espoused values, and I knew I had to change the way I was advising so that I could empower the students to run, lead, and learn from their organization.

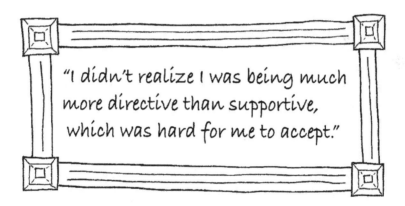

"I didn't realize I was being much more directive than supportive, which was hard for me to accept."

**Making changes took work.** It required better one-on-one meetings with the president to make sure she was knowledgeable and confident about the purposes and where we were going. It required joint meetings with the president and executive board members to help them develop their positions so that they would be positive role models for future members of the organization. It required providing resources for the members. Finally, it required promoting and supporting discussion and decision-making.

Now that a year has gone by, things are going much better. The members have more autonomy and ownership of their organization. I also spend less time on the nitty-gritty, and more time on the larger, long-term needs of the organization. **Throughout this past year I have been more cautious and thoughtful of the way I approach student decision-making and learning in order to be more supportive, and I intend to continue doing this as an advisor.** I am thankful that this situation caused me to be more aware of my advising. The changes I have made are bringing me closer to my view of a "good" support/direction balance and working within my values on organization advising.

 *Mike Giacalone is the Student Activities Program Coordinator at Rhode Island College working with Greek Life and Student Organizations. Mike spends his free time volunteering with Sigma Phi Epsilon, watching way too much Food Network, and reading. You can connect with him on Twitter @mikegiacalone.*

# creating CARE-ful connections

Creating Care-ful Connections – Candace DeAngelis

In the early days of my career, I remember being so confident in my ability to be a great advisor to students. As a new professional, I served on every committee possible to expand my experience and build my resume, and I was always the first one in and the last one to leave. I was so determined to teach students what I had learned and to help them be successful. I was prepared to change lives.

**The truth is, I was naïve.** I thought organizations were going to form, storm, norm and perform in a neat, little progression and that students would develop interdependence and establish mature relationships just as the vectors I learned about had indicated. My academic studies had given me the foundation of theory, and I thought all I had to do was take the theory and put it to practice. **After many interactions with students and countless conversations with colleagues, I realized this was going to be harder than I thought.**

Weeks, days, and hours were gone in a flash and my 'open door' policy became a revolving door of constant problems: issues within organizations, relationship drama, financial woes. It was making it very difficult to do 'my job.' **Then it occurred to me that perhaps it wasn't my IQ that would make me successful in working with student**

**organizations, but my EQ or ability to be emotionally intelligent, that would make me a good practitioner.** I not only needed to learn how to perceive students' emotions, but I also needed to teach them to express and manage their own emotions. I knew that if I could help students be more aware of others and encourage them to establish strong relationships with other student leaders, they would be able to use those skills to act appropriately and successfully in challenging situations. I needed to empower them to create empathic connections with one another.

In the thick of the spring semester, we tend to get very overwhelmed by our schedules and our students. I will admit that by mid-April, I sometimes secretly daydream of Commencement because of the little break it provides between Graduation and Orientation. **In times of stress, it's easy to dismiss the problems of our students and get frustrated by their lack of follow through.** Perhaps it's endless cups of coffee we consume, or maybe it's the 14th day in a row of working 14-hour days, but spring semester is enough to put any Student Affairs professional a little on edge. Here are a few things that, even in the busiest of times, under the most stressful situations, help us be better advisors to our students and help them to help each other.

> "In times of stress, it's easy to dismiss the problems of our students and get frustrated by their lack of follow through."

## Teach them to listen. Really listen.

I admit, sometimes it takes all of my being not to roll my eyes at a student who responds to my cordial, "How are you?" with their whole life story. Don't they know that I have 50 million things to do... before lunch...and that I don't have time to listen to them tell me about the drama between them and their BFF for the fourth time?

Remember that they are confiding in you because they trust you and they respect you as their advisor, and in turn, they should expect that same level of trust and respect from one another. Try your best to listen to the students and hear between the lines. **You never know when you might hear a cry for help or get an opportunity for a teachable moment.**

Teach them to be there for each other with a listening, non-judgmental ear. I always tell students they have 2 ears and one mouth because they should listen twice as much as they speak. Make time for them or schedule an appointment when you know you can be truly present with them and remind them to do the same with others.

### Encourage them to hurry up... and wait.

I used to get upset and annoyed when students on the programming board would not turn in projects by the due date. I wanted them to be as organized as I had learned to be. Don't they know how much easier life is with color-coded post-it notes? If they don't meet your deadlines, it's often not because they don't care, but because life got in the way and they were afraid to tell you or ask for an extension for fear that they might disappoint you.

Have candid conversations with your students about how much is on their plate and advise them to only take on things they can handle. Be patient with students and communicate to them the importance of meeting deadlines, but be open and flexible whenever possible. Teaching them to prioritize the importance of each delegated task in advance, and communicate with one another on the things they volunteer for, will certainly bring peace to any organization of over-achievers.

### Remind them to laugh... even when they want to cry.

According to Tal Ben-Shahar in his book *Happier*, happiness is the ultimate currency. Student Affairs is not going to make you a millionaire, but you can be very rich with happiness in this field. Instead of asking ourselves, "Am I Happy?", which Shahar notes is an unhelpful question, we should be asking ourselves, "How can I be happier?". One of the best ways I try to find happiness is through laughter.

Have you ever smiled at yourself in the mirror when you are in a bad mood? I have and I encourage students to do it too! You will laugh at how silly you feel and it will actually make you feel better.

When working with student organizations, it is so important to enjoy the students and be a member of their team. Laughing together will show the students your human side and will help you build stronger relationships with them. You can be professional and still have a great time, and the humor will create a great relief from the stress and pressure.

**Thank them often and teach them to be thankful.**

Recognizing and rewarding others for a job well done teaches appreciation and respect. As an advisor, modeling this behavior can go a long way among student organizations. Student leaders and club members want to feel appreciated. They want to know their ideas are heard and their efforts matter. Be sure to tell them how much you appreciate the work they do – it will mean more to them than you will ever know.

 *Candace currently serves as the Associate Director of Student Activities and New Student Orientation at Eastern Connecticut State University. She strives to challenge and support students in her work with orientation and leadership programs, and assists student leaders in recognizing their limitless potential. Follow Candace on Twitter @chdeangelis.*

# NOT 'JUST' AN ADVISOR

Not "Just" an Advisor – Ryan Bye

I'll admit it, advising is not something that I have always valued. I often considered it "just" being an advisor. However, supervision? Now that's where it was at, in my mind. Supervision seemed to hold a more serious tone in my life and appeared to be more credible. **As I have moved on in my career, I realized that I had supervision and advising in a false dichotomy.** I think Student Affairs as a field creates this false dichotomy between supervising and advising through our interview questions, division of responsibilities, and prioritization. Luckily, I have come to love advising and have seen the power it has in the role of the educational process.

Over my past two years at Valparaiso University, I have had the privilege to serve in a variety of advising roles. My position in residence life affords me the opportunity to advise groups within my hall, but right now I want to focus on other opportunities: **fraternity advising and the National Residence Hall Honorary.**

This past year, I have worked on the Mentor Board for the Indiana Zeta chapter of Sigma Phi Epsilon at Valparaiso University. I am unaffiliated with any fraternity and so when I was approached and agreed to do this, I had no idea what I was getting into. **Since accepting, however, I have gained knowledge about learning a culture, offering**

**insight, and fueling an idea.** I was brought in specifically to help the Vice President of Programming with the group's big annual SigEp Christmas philanthropy.

The student and I were one of the first mentor pairs to start meeting on a regular basis, and it was awesome. Other pairs started meeting, mentors reaching out to mentees, mentees reaching out to mentors, and the program being successfully used. I would be remiss if I did not say there was a learning curve for me – as a non-member, I had a lot to learn about this chapter. My priority was to learn how the student I was working with saw their culture, where he thought he fit in, and how could he help make it better. **We spent a lot of time talking about goals; I learned that the ideas I offered were taken very seriously and acted on often.**

> "We spent a lot of time talking about goals; I learned that the ideas I offered were taken very seriously and acted on often."

Another advising role I have taken on is within our National Residence Hall Honorary (NRHH) chapter. This group is based in and funded by the department I work for. This group has undergone some major changes in the past five years. It has wavered between being a club for overly involved RAs, to reaching out to our residential population. On a campus that has a three-year live-on requirement, I see the value that this group brings, but at times they have struggled to see that themselves.

As their advisor, I have had to work a lot with the executive board of the group (which at times has been the really, really, really overly involved students) to figure out ways to motivate their chapter, have themselves place some level of priority into the organization, and figure out what they want this organization to be known for. **Sometimes I have had to let them fail and then discuss with them the reasons they failed.** I needed them to learn that having an executive board that wasn't committed to the group was not a sustainable option. On the other side of that, there have been times where I have had to truly guide them because we were planning an event my supervisor, the Dean of Students, and the Vice President of Student Affairs were all going to be at. With this group, I have had to learn to be okay with where the group is at and celebrate every small step they take towards living out their vision.

**Each of these groups needed something different from me, and I had something different to learn from each of these groups.** There have been moments where I know I have struggled as an advisor. I have missed learning moments I could have had with an executive board, I probably came to a meeting with too much emotion on my sleeve, and there are times I could have been more prepared. I chose to believe through all of that that the students and I have learned how to be better community members. We have learned how to help each other out, how to work relentlessly towards our goals, and how to move forward. I have seen the benefits of advising.

This year, when I was deciding if my schedule would allow me to remain the advisor of NRHH, and the executive board heard of the possibility that I would not be the advisor, they all reached out to me asking me to stay. I recently was also asked to stay on the mentor board for Sigma Phi Epsilon. I know that I am a stronger professional, supervisor, and leader because of these experiences. **We can choose to be just an advisor, but we have to remember that advising is so much more than that. It has the power to change not only our students' lives, but our own.**

*Ryan is a second year Residential Learning Coordinator @ValpoResLife. He found a sense of home in his undergrad through his involvement with Res Life. He is passionate about event planning, advising & supervision, and creating a sense of community. Ryan believes there could never be enough coffee or wine to drink, books to read, or words to say. Connect with Ryan on Twitter @ByeByeRyan*

# Privilege, Power & Advising

Privilege, Power, & Advising – Brian Lackman

Since my first day of graduate school I have been truly excited and invigorated by working with student organizations. Over the past seven years, I have had the fortune to work with wonderfully dynamic student organizations and leaders, ranging from traditional student organizations (academic student organizations, multicultural student organizations, etc.) to unique and fun organizations (humans vs. zombies, the lumberjack club, and more) Student organizations, to me, not only represent the best of our campus community but they also keep me engaged and focused. **However, no group had been as engaging for me to work with until I was able to work with a local sorority (or as they are known at Davidson College, an eating house).** As a white, male, student affairs professional, these remarkable women have helped me to grow in my awareness of my identity and taught me how to further my voice.

While not being a member of a Greek lettered organization myself, from the onset of my career I was fortunate to be surrounded by truly wonderful and motivational friends and colleagues who exposed me to the power of the values based movement. These women challenged any presumptions I had developed earlier in my life about sororities, as my only exposure prior was that portrayed in Hollywood, which does not do justice to the sorority movement. **I saw the power that this approach had on multiple communities and how it impacted the**

**campus' ethos.** As a male who has spent his entire life growing up in an environment around strong women I strive to be an advocate for feminism. All of these experiences lead to me being presented with an opportunity to get involved in Greek Life and I was excitedly pointed toward serving as an advisor to one of the eating houses.

When I started my role as an advisor, the organization had been through a revolutionary few months. As a local organization, they have a great deal of autonomy in decision making, and are regularly exploring their identity on campus as its members develop. One example comes from the eating house being approached by male members of the community who initiated a conversation about changing the organization from a women's organization to a mixed-gender one. Simultaneously, in the light of many national conversations around sexual violence, the women were actively working to find ways to support their members who had been the victims of violence. **With all of this change happening, I knew that I had to evolve my advisory approach.**

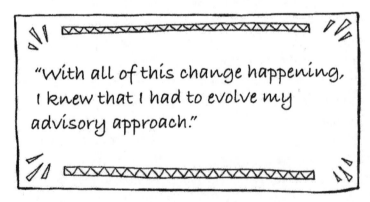

"With all of this change happening, I knew that I had to evolve my advisory approach."

**I found that in order to engage the members of the house as honestly and effectively as possible, I had to be very proactive in addressing my identity and privilege.** This proactive approach helped me to develop a rapport with the women, but more importantly to do something that I should have already been doing in any of my advising experiences in order to be as effective as possible to support this organization: **addressing my privileges, presumptions, and understanding that I brought into this role.** In my initial conversations with the women, I acknowledged my privileges and positional power outright in order to effectively deconstruct barriers and work toward developing a mutual understanding. I realized that despite my pro-feminist viewpoint as a person and as a professional, I needed to acknowledge that my masculinity, and my view as a staff member, brought with it a very different framework than the women of the house. I had to address the issues surrounding my spheres of power and influence as a white male and as an administrator. **I asked the woman I served, how I could support them as individuals, and as an organization, both personally and in my advisory capacity and leverage my privileges in order to be a better advocate for the organization.** The students appeared taken aback by this and voiced their appreciation for my transparency. The women discussed that one of the greatest challenges they were experiencing was not only trying to find their voice, but having their voice be affirmed.

Combining this approach with strengths-based coaching allowed me to engage the women more effectively than I had been able to do with other organizations to this point. While I am still new to advising Greek organizations, my work with this organization has taught me a lot about the need for effective and intentional advising with all student organizations. **It is important that as student affairs professionals we are actively and regularly checking our privileges and sphere of influence when working in advisory capacities in order to make more meaningful educational and developmental climates.**

*Brian Lackman is a scholar-practitioner who has interest in developing our field's understanding of new and under-discussed topics as well as working towards making a positive impact on campus, which currently include multicultural education for new professionals as well as Asexuality. Currently, Brian serves as an Area Coordinator & the Coordinator of Residential Curriculum at Davidson College where he also serves as a Safe Space Facilitator and an advisor to student groups. Twitter: @BrianRLackman*

# STRONG WOMEN, LEADERS.

Strong Women, Strong Leaders — Kimberly White

Advising is one of my favorite parts of the work I do. As a Campus Advisor to the ladies of the Alabama Alpha chapter of the Pi Beta Phi Fraternity for Women, I have been so fortunate to observe a group of strong women hone their leadership skills and work collectively to fulfill the values of the organization. I view my chapter like family and am so proud to watch each member grow over four years.

My work as a Campus Advisor typically involves collaborating with our chapter leaders, the Executive Council, to provide opportunities for career and leadership development in both one-on-one and group settings. Much of the programming is similar to the campus-wide initiatives that I oversee, such as workshops on resume building, but the process is truly tailored to the chapter and each of its members. **I've noticed a positive change in our chapter's communication skills, confidence levels, and overall happiness with Pi Phi over the past year, and I do believe that our chapter's combined efforts to focus on developing strong leaders has been a major contributor to our success.**

In addition, I've witnessed an increase in confidence levels among our chapter, something I attribute to both our development efforts and a strong sense of empowerment and support. Sisterhood runs deep in our organization, and by having a female professional on campus to offer encouragement and work closely with the chapter, we have strengthened our ties with one another even further. When I discuss my work with Pi Phi, I always tell others that I've enjoyed so many more gains from my affiliation with the chapter than I could ever return, but many of the younger members have expressed their enthusiasm about having an on-campus advisor to turn to. **Career and leadership development can be a daunting task for our students to take on, but a focus on collective learning and support has caused many of our chapter members to apply for opportunities that they wouldn't have felt confident enough to consider otherwise.** Advising student organizations is never easy, but this is why I can truly say that I love what I do.

Here are some ways that advisors could foster career development in their student organizations. While these activities may vary, these ideas could be tailored to fit a number of student groups.

1. **Office Hours**: I set aside one hour each week for Pi Phi, giving our chapter members an opportunity to drop by and discuss topics such as internship opportunities, resume reviews, mock interviewing, or professionally communicating their Pi Phi accomplishments and projects. It's been a great way to provide

individualized attention to the chapter, as well as make each woman feel supported on campus. I'm also able to get to know each member individually, so I can better assist and encourage them to consider different types of professional opportunities.

2. **Attending and Sponsoring Events**: By attending events put on by our student organizations, we are showing active interest in the values and principles that they promote, as well as providing an additional opportunity to bond with the group. I've found that informal conversations with members of the group at tailgates and philanthropy events have led to more successful one-on-one meetings because I get to know the chapter better and can tailor my approach to fit its needs.

3. **Culture of Support**: This goes hand in hand with attending events put on by the organization, but it's a crucial part of leadership and career development for advisors. In addition to holding office hours and showing my Pi Phi support at different events, I am always aware of my language and attitudes when working with the group. I push them to apply for opportunities that pique their interest, provide them with support

through the application process for different leadership positions, celebrate with them when they embark on new endeavors, and console them when they are turned away from a project. Each woman in the chapter knows that I have her back no matter the outcome, and it allows for us to have honest discussions about her professional pursuits and her unique skill set. I understand how tough this topic can be for our students, and I could not truly foster strong leaders without supporting them.

I encourage student organization advisors to consider implementing career development into your advising model, even if it involves simply mentioning the vast number of leadership, experiential learning, and co-curricular opportunities to your groups. They will bring back skills that can truly support the development of your organization and the group at large.

 *Kimberly White is the Internship Coordinator for the rise3 Initiative at Birmingham-Southern College, an experiential learning and critical reflection opportunity for students in the domains of faculty-student research, internships, and service-learning. She also serves as the BSC Campus Advisor to the Pi Beta Phi Fraternity for Women, Alabama Alpha chapter. Twitter: @whiteoi*

INTERNATIONAL STUDENT ORGANIZATIONS
*Learning Stories + Giving Voice*

International Student Organizations: Learning Stories and Giving Voice – Amy Corron

In exploring different areas of student involvement work, I wanted to advise a student organization that I connected with personally and shared similar undergraduate experiences with. I completed the majority of my undergraduate experience abroad at the University of St. Andrews in Scotland and was therefore thrilled when the Miami University International Student Organization asked me to be a co-advisor of their organization. **I was excited to work with a new population of students and have opportunities to explore the similarities and differences in our joint experiences as international students.** I felt familiar with the international students' unique needs and was motivated towards providing them with advising, mentorship, and resources.

We quickly hit some rough bumps in the beginning. I initially went into the experience with my general advising philosophy and style, which is relatively hands-off and focuses on a student-driven experience. I also have clear conversations about expectations and accountability for both student leaders and myself. With the International Student Organization, I was beginning to get frustrated with students' lack of independent action and follow-through on delegated tasks. They, similarly, were unhappy with my hands-off style and were looking for me to be more involved in all of their activities. The organization worked as a collective group where members made joint decisions and worked on projects and programming as a whole. **Once I realized the differences in working style, I revised my advising approach and joined in on their collective efforts.**

I also developed an understanding of the stories of each member individually, and not just a handful of executive board officers. As an organization, they were home to all international students on campus from a large variety of home countries, cultures, and ethnicities. **We had students from all over the globe, and each member had their own unique background which influenced how they participated in the group and what further needs they had on campus.** In making relationships with each member, I better understood how they approached organization tasks and how they played an active role in the group.

Despite individual cultural differences, as a whole, the international students felt they did not have adequate resources on our campus. There was a large disconnect between international and domestic students and they did not feel integrated into the campus community by their peers, faculty, or staff. **They also felt there was little they could do to make positive change for themselves and other international students in this area.** Together, we learned about advocacy and how to act as an advocate for the international students within our spheres of influence. I encouraged them to become actively involved in the Diversity Affairs Council, the student governing body for student identity groups, and make their needs known to other student leaders. I met regularly with the club leaders and the Director of the International Student office to review these issues and give voice to their experiences with upper administration. When a new student center was opened, the organization was granted office space with the main purpose to be able to meet one-on-one with other international students and provide peer support. We continued to host programs over the school break periods for social interaction and fun and recreation for international students who did not travel and remained on campus. Slowly but surely, we were able to make sustainable positive change, and the organization members felt more empowered about their identities as Miami University students.

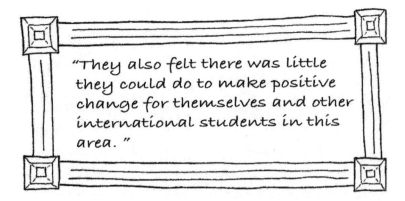

"They also felt there was little they could do to make positive change for themselves and other international students in this area."

We ended our two year advising relationship on a high note – the International Student Organization won the Outstanding Organization award and I was honored to receive the Outstanding Graduate Advisor award at the university's annual student organization recognition ceremony. I was so proud that the organization was recognized at a high level for their incredible work and very humbled that they nominated me on behalf of my advising efforts. **Co-advising the International Student Organization was a bright highlight in my graduate program that helped me learn about myself as an advisor and provided opportunities to empower students to create positive change while advocating on their behalf.**

As I settled into my first full-time job in New York, I was pulled back to Miami when I read a letter to the editor of the student newspaper from a faculty member lamenting the growing number of international students due to their poor academic performance and lack of integration into the community. In one sentence, the faculty member referred to the international students in their classes as "dead weight." **My heart hurt for my former students as I conceptualized the meaning of these words and their oppressive impact on all international students at Miami.**

I was encouraged in the days following, seeing a response from one of my former faculty colleagues and a strong social media presence of support from other Student Affairs graduate students. **I was even more overjoyed to see the International Student Organization plan and**

**execute a social media response asking Miami community members to post pictures tagged with #WeAreMiami describing stories of what it means to be an international student and what it means to know international students at Miami.** The responses that followed from students, faculty, and staff were individually and collectively powerful. Each picture had a different story that overall contributed to a sense of support and community. I was able to participate from afar and let the students know how proud I was of their choice in action and continued ability to advocate for themselves and their community.

The International Student Organization continues to thrive with dedicated co-advisors who deeply care about international student well-being and success. I am fortunate to have had the opportunity to work with such a passionate, bright, and kind group of students who continue to give me inspiration and purpose in my work.

*Amy Corron is the Assistant Director of Student Activities in the Rensselaer Union at Rensselaer Polytechnic Institute in Troy, New York. She also keeps a side hustle as the Asst. Women's Rugby Coach at Siena College (go Saints!). Her interests include social justice education, student affairs assessment, rugby, CrossFit, amateur cooking, and coffee drinking. She has never eaten a piece of cheese she didn't like. Connect with her on Twitter @amersy*

## I Will Advise, But I Won't Always Agree.

I Will Advise, But I Won't Always Agree – Dr. Bradley Karasik

Without a doubt, every advisor reading this feels that they are advising students, groups, and organizations with the best interest of the students in mind. We enjoy collaborating with them and watching them develop. **We take joy when they succeed and we are disappointed when things don't go as planned.**

> "We take joy when they succeed and we are disappointed when things don't go as planned."

Our memories want us to believe that we expend the same amount of energy and passion with everyone who crosses our path. As professionals, we surely follow the same policies and procedures with all. As long as what is presented does not violate any institutional or governmental laws, we are wholeheartedly committed. Playing favorites is not an option.

Unfortunately, **we sometimes choose to play favorites without even realizing it.** As humans we connect with some students, causes, and groups more than others. We must accept this fact and figure out how we can put our personal self aside to be our best professional self. **Each student leader, group and organization we encounter needs to feel as if what they are working on means as much to us as it does to them.** In all of my years advising student leaders and organizations, this has been one of my biggest struggles. I believe I have been able to (mostly) overcome this difficult challenge. Before I share the methods that have worked for me, let's look at two scenarios that should sound familiar.

## Scenario #1

Sunshine is the president of a large organization that is committed to a cause that you strongly believe in. **She always meets deadlines, is a pleasant person to work with, and continually thanks you for all of your help.** If/when Sunshine is faced with obstacles or challenges, you empower her to work through them and assure her that you will do all you can to make sure the organization reaches its goals. You genuinely want Sunshine to succeed and her organization to reach its goals. It will personally distress you if Sunshine and/or the organization are not as successful as they set out to be.

## Scenario #2

Trouble has just created a new organization on campus that stands for a cause you absolutely disagree with. **Trouble has an abrasive personality, always tries to circumvent the system, and feels she knows how to do things without any help.** Trouble can't be bothered with policies and procedures and waits until the final moments on every decision. The only time Trouble engages with you is when she runs into roadblocks and expects you to remove them immediately. If you are successful in removing the barrier, your hard work is not appreciated. You do what is required to help Trouble and her organization, but are not really invested in the successes or failures they may face.

Each of us has crossed paths with some variation of the scenarios above. It may be Sunshine running an organization with a cause you dislike or Trouble running an organization you believe in. In all cases, the same challenge remains. **How do you advocate and advise wholeheartedly when your heart is not in it?** Are you truly able to be equitable in all scenarios? Hopefully your answer is honest and you realize you do your best to be fair and recognize the challenges in doing so.

In practice, to effectively advise student leaders and organizations with all my vigor, I needed to find an internal motivation that made me want to see them succeed. **The**

**motivation I used was to move beyond the individual or organization and achieve satisfaction through my growth process.** Demanding student leaders gave me the opportunity to refine my skills in dealing with difficult people. When an organizational cause went against my beliefs I was challenged to focus on the process and not the cause.

Using the techniques above positively impacted my relationship with Trouble and her organization. A day dealing with Trouble was a day I grew as a person. A day dealing with her organization was a day that I grew as a professional. **By embracing these growth opportunities I began to look forward to working with Trouble and her organization as much as Sunshine and her group.**

Sunshine every day would become boring. Sometimes we all need a little Trouble to keep us on our toes.

 *Dr. Bradley Karasik is an experienced professional in both the non-profit and higher education sectors. He conducts academic research on the impact education has on earning mobility and lectures on leadership development and community building. His twitter handle is @bkarasik.*

# ᵂᵃ aren't we so nice? ᵂᵃ

Aren't We So Nice? – Dr. Christine Wilson

Sanford advanced the now time-tested concept of "challenge and support" in the early 1960s. He asserted that there must be a balance of supportive and challenging aspects in college students' lives in order to maximize growth and development. Challenges are activities that push students beyond their current competency. Support is an environmental function that encourages growth to happen in a safe way. **Too much challenge leads to frustration, and too much support impedes learning.** (For great examples of operationalized challenges and supports, see Roark's article in the Summer 1989 NASPA Journal.)

This theory has served many of my fellow advisors and me well over the past 25 years. It is an adaptable theory that can apply to our diverse student organization leaders; it is flexible and inclusive. Challenges and supports will vary from person to person, so we as advisors can adapt to our individual student leaders. In fact, getting to know the things that challenge and support our student leaders is a great way to building advising relationships.

## Under challenged and over supported means less growth

Few advisors will argue with these concepts - in theory. As a daily practice? Well, that is another matter. As early as 1966, Sanford asserted that colleges do not challenge students sufficiently. I agree. *I think we over support our student leaders and under challenge them.*

Student leaders are definitely challenged, by a myriad of issues, including member commitment issues, time management, and budgeting complications. They are also challenged by their own lack of skills, lack of experience, and personal weaknesses. All of these challenges can promote growth, and help students broaden their perspectives and build their skills.

## "Nice" as a barrier to growth

There will only be growth if we challenge student leaders to learn from their own failures and shortcomings. But sometimes we do not challenge them, we only support them. For some reason, we land in "nice." Why? Advising can be a truly rewarding endeavor. Helping students and witnessing their achievements is exhilarating. Do we perceive that challenging student leaders will hurt our relationships with them? Are we afraid that we won't be seen as good advisors? Are we afraid that the folks "above us" will critique our work? Is this why we tell student leaders that they are great even when we should be holding them accountable for poor leadership? Could this be why we sometimes do their student organization work for them when we should be letting them fail?

## Advisors: Know your own challenges and supports

This is why Sanford's theory is so relevant, even forty years later. **While we are challenging and supporting our student leaders, we need to understand what we as advisors need to feel supported and challenged.** It is a personal development issue for us as advisors. Maybe you feel comfortable confronting (challenging) a student leader who handled a situation poorly, maybe you don't. If you don't, you need to learn how to do that so that the student isn't deprived of a growth opportunity. And maybe it makes you a little nauseous to think about cancelling an event because the students aren't finishing their work, and so that is why you do the work for them.

Caveat: **The reality of an advisor's work is that it doesn't happen in a vacuum.** Each advisor has personal challenges and supports, but the work environment has its own challenges and supports. Perhaps you want to let students fail because they haven't done the work, but money has been invested and your supervisor would not support you in letting the event fail. Perhaps the risks of a student planned event become too great for the students to handle, and you step in to help them manage the risks on behalf of the university. In these situations, student growth might not be maximized, but there is still room for growth if these issues are discussed with students so that they can cognitively, if not experientially, be challenged.

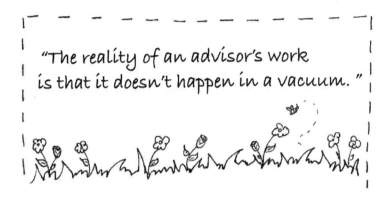

"The reality of an advisor's work is that it doesn't happen in a vacuum."

## The hard road for the advisors (not being "nice") can lead to growth for the students

I once pushed a student organization to cancel a conference they were planning because the leaders had not fulfilled the responsibilities that they had defined for themselves. Some of them were extremely angry. Some understood. Some begged me to understand that they were students, and shouldn't have to shoulder the burden of a conference on their own. I agreed, but reminded them that, first of all, we had already considered the burden and they chose to shoulder it, and secondly, I would not do their work for them. My biggest critics were my colleagues, some of whom couldn't believe I could be so direct and so mean (the opposite of "nice"). I am not saying that this was easy, or that it would even be possible at all institutions. I do think it was the most educational thing to do for the students. Years later, I saw one of the student leaders in that organization at a conference. She had become an event planner. **She told me that the cancelling of that conference was the most meaningful moment in her career preparation.** She said that, in retrospect, she was glad I didn't "let them get away with slacking," and that my actions helped her see that an advisor could help students even when an advisor wasn't "nice."

That's the thing. **When we do not challenge our students– when our challenges get in the way of challenging our students–we are impeding their growth.** We may even be "un-educating" them. Take the risk. Worry less about being "nice." Face your own challenges so that you can you can do better by your students.

 *Christine Wilson serves as the Director of Student Activities at UConn. She also supervises the Office of Fraternity and Sorority Life and five Cultural Centers. She teaches in the Higher Education and Student Affairs master's program on a variety of subjects.*

# I HAVE NO idea WHAT I'M DOING

I Have No Idea What I'm Doing – Casey Mulcare

I had nailed it. After a small foray into the world of campus space reservations after graduate school, I had landed my ideal gig, only a year later than anticipated. I was back in student activities and working with a programming board – I could not have been happier. I was back in my natural work environment where my strengths could really shine. I had a variety of experiences from undergraduate, graduate, and professional work to pull from and some great ideas I wanted to implement. Most of all, I was determined to be really, really good at advising this group. **I was going to make the most of this opportunity and show how ready I was for the job.**

I realized, in my first year back in Org Advising since graduate school, **that I had NO idea what I was doing.** It's not to say I couldn't do the work, but the work didn't come easy. The shift into being the "word of wisdom" or the "final say" for a group of students who knew more about their roles and what my role should be was not easy. I messed up, a lot. **From budgeting to organizational management to event planning, I don't think I had one week where there wasn't something I noticed I could have done better.** I had yet to get used to balancing the multiple pieces of advising a programming board, along with my other job responsibilities, and little things kept slipping through the cracks.

Don't get me wrong, I'm still here (as of writing this anyway). I might be exaggerating a tad on the glaring discrepancies, **but the truth remains that advisors put a lot of pressure on themselves to have the answers and be the expert.** Many of us have the advanced degrees, life experiences, and training that our students do not, so we should be able to overcome any bump in the road, right? I'm here to say that that's wrong. **We don't have to have the answers, and we don't have to be afraid to ask for help.** We can be wrong, and that's OK.

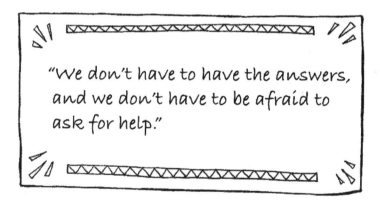

> "We don't have to have the answers, and we don't have to be afraid to ask for help."

For me, I had to be very honest with myself, and with my students. I became comfortable with telling them, "Hey, I'm new here, so it's going to take me some time to get to know the ropes". Guess what? **They responded to that honesty.** Really well, in fact. They helped me while I helped them, and as the year went on, through some storming (both winter weather related and otherwise), life got easier. We were able to look back on some of our missteps as learning opportunities and the group was able to gain confidence going into Maprilay (March-April-May insanity. Not my phrase, though I wish it was).

I know I can get caught up on the smallest missteps of an event or process that could have gone better. It's easy to forget the successes that the group had achieved in countless other events. Many of our students do the same thing, spending more time worrying about the one plant that didn't sprout in proverbial field of thriving growth. **It's important to reflect back on the positives, recognize the effort and the learning that went into that event (on both the students' end and my own), and look for ways to add those ingredients for success into future efforts.**

This goes for supporting our colleagues as well. We all work in offices where we have an influx of events going on at the same time of year, and we'll probably hear more of what's going wrong behind the scenes than we will about how well the event actually will turn out. I know after a rough week of Homecoming (my first as an advisor), the congratulations from the office staff and a simple card from my supervisor made a world of difference on my outlook of the events that took place. And guess what? **All the little things I thought were major issues, nobody else remembers.** The students and staff remember the successes of a new Spirit Week initiative the students championed, and had no idea about the group's struggles with logistics behind the scenes.

As I went into my first Springfest week at Bridgewater, complete with a headlining comedy show and carnival, I told myself the following: I will take a bit of solace in knowing that I'm not in this role alone, and I'm not expected to have all the answers. We will inevitably have hiccups, as any program will, and plans will go astray, but the show will go on. I know my students will support me just as I've tried to support them throughout the year. **As advisors, we work hard to provide a learning experience for our student leaders, and an essential part of that is to learn on our end too.** Every student leader has their "first time" at a program, where they'll learn and grow from the experience to make it more successful the next time. **It's all right for the advisors to have that experience too.**

*Casey is in his first year as the Coordinator for Student Programming at Bridgewater State University, overseeing the Program Council and Bridgewater's weekend programming series. When he's not at work, Casey can be found eating pizza, drinking too much coffee and being an overall obnoxious Bostonian. @CGMulcare on twitter*

# navigating the REVOLVING DOOR of club leadership

Navigating the Revolving Door of Club Leadership –
Christopher Conzen

Community college students are typically less likely to participate in on-campus leadership activities than their peers at the four-year universities (Miller et al., 2005). Fifty-nine percent of community college students are enrolled part-time, compared to the 27% of students at four-year universities (National Center for Education Statistics [NCES], 2010). Community college students are more likely to work 20 or more hours per week at off-campus locations, with less than 20% of students not working at all (Orozco & Cauthen, 2009). **After balancing academic responsibilities, employment and family obligations, community college students are left with little time to engage in leadership skills development opportunities on campus.** For this reason, clubs and organizations can serve as a critical link to student involvement for community college students.

While student organizations at the community college appear similarly to their counterparts at senior colleges, the constraints on student availability combined with the rapid turnover in leadership positions carry unique challenges for the community college advisor. The most successful organizations tend to be the ones that connect to an academic program, as the students see these organizations as an opportunity to connect with their professors outside of the classroom. The academic connections also provide the faculty advisor with the benefit of tying what's learned in the classroom to the activities planned outside. **In this way, many organizations serve as almost a laboratory for the curricular experience.**

Student organizations on the community college level tend to require advisors to be more hands-on and directive. Student activity in these organizations can often be limited to built-in common hours (mid-day blocks of time where classes are not scheduled to allow for involvement in activities). **The success of student organizations may often rely on the work of advisors behind the scenes, such as planning programs or putting together funding request paperwork.** The frequent turnover of student leaders in organizations often leaves the advisor as the one stationary element during the numerous transitions.

One of the benefits for advisors in community colleges is the lack of a **"publish or perish"** environment for faculty. In fact, involvement in some way in the college community can often be one of the factors used to award tenure to full-time faculty. This leaves faculty with more quality time to spend with student organizations and to work with the members in developing activities. This can also mean that the role of the activities professional can be as much supporting the faculty advisor as the students in the organizations.

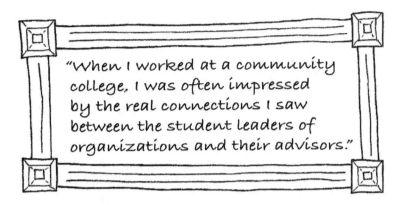

"When I worked at a community college, I was often impressed by the real connections I saw between the student leaders of organizations and their advisors."

**When I worked at a community college, I was often impressed by the real connections I saw between the student leaders of organizations and their advisors.** The advisors frequently went above and beyond the "call of duty" and there were even moments where the advisor was the only factor keeping a club active during long periods of transition. These faculty members were frequently rewarded by the gestures of adulation at our end of the year awards ceremonies. What I think differentiates the community college organization advisor from one at a senior college is that the former is often the heart of the organization, bringing life to a rewarding experience for students, no matter how briefly they might be engaged.

 *Chris Conzen is a leadership educator with 15 years in student affairs. Chris currently serves as the Assistant Dean of Student Life at LIM College in New York City. Prior to his assignment at LIM College, Chris spent 8 ½ years leading the activities office at a community college.*

Never the Same Day Twice – Jeff Pelletier

I've been fortunate to serve as a student organization advisor for the entirety of my career in Student Affairs. I work with three different groups: a men's fraternity, the running club, and our veteran student organization. To say they're all different is a bit of an understatement. **Nowhere in my work does the phrase "meet them where they are" apply more than in my interactions with student organizations.** Notice I did not say "meet them where they're at," which is intentional. That's terrible, terrible grammar.

My "first" organization is Delta Tau Delta. I began working with this group when they were recolonizing on campus, my first fall as a new professional. I was assigned to be their chapter advocate, a staff member assigned to a new Greek colony to help with the myriad of challenges that comes along with starting a new chapter on campus. I do not have enough room to list all of the learning I have gained from the nearly 200 men who have come through the chapter in my time as advisor. **I do know that whenever the active members ask me when I'll stop advising, the answer is usually "when I stop learning, or when you abandon our values."** So far, so good.

Being a runner, it was a natural fit for me to add the running club to my advisees. This club is fairly self-sufficient, and has a volatile membership, so my interaction is primarily with the officers. I rarely have the opportunity to interact with the club's casual members, or even those consistent members who simply seek a good workout and a connection back to the cross-country or track teams they left in high school. I make an effort to attend (and participate in!) their annual intro to campus run during Welcome Week. I do my best to keep up with the second pace group, knowing my days of running with the front of the back are long behind me. I enjoy being able to run side by side with students half my age, and being able to support their community as best I can. We've forged a wonderful relationship with the director of the Columbus Marathon, which has opened up opportunities for many of our runners to participate in the half or full marathon on a student-friendly budget. **I'm not "needed" for much more than a signature on any of a dozen race registration forms or travel requests to meets, but I always know I'm welcome to join them on the plaza of the union for a daily workout.**

Serving as co-advisor for Vets for Vets is a newer venture, **but probably one of my greatest honors.** The stories and experiences of this group of students are unlike any other organization, and I'm fortunate to call them peers as a veteran myself. When I stopped by their event on Veteran's Day this year, I met the president of the organization for the first time – he was elected 6 months before. I apologized for not making regular meetings or events, to which he responded that I was exactly the advisor they needed: completely hands off, but completely accessible when needed. **While I thought I was letting them down, it turns out I was giving them all the space they wanted to do their own thing.**

"While I thought I was letting them down, it turns out I was giving them all the space they wanted to do their own thing."

I've needed to bend my advisory style to meet what each group needs, which can make some advisors feel a bit scatterbrain, myself included. **Meeting each group where they are allows me to not just make a contribution, but make the contribution that is needed.** I attend meetings twice a week for Delta, less than monthly for the Running Club, and never for Vets for Vets. As it turns out, that's what each of them wants and needs. But the relationships are no less meaningful among the students involved in each. Countless recommendation letters, references for jobs, and one fight through cancer for a two-term president of the running club have shown me that no matter my involvement, it is appreciated, needed, and necessary.

 *Jeff spent 21 years as an "army brat," and another eight years as Naval Officer and civilian contractor. He currently works for the Ohio State University, where he oversees Ohio Union operations, and advises Delta Tau Delta Fraternity, the OSU Running Club, and Vets for Vets. When the weather cooperates, he is almost always out for a run. You can connect with Jeff on Twitter at @JeffBC94*

# You Can. / I WON'T.

You can. I won't. – Joe Ginese

## "You know what? Go for it. You can. I won't."

You've no doubt have been in your office with your club/class/organization officers sitting with unbridled excitement about this FUN and NEW idea they have to raise money/party/bring the class together. In this meeting, you sit back with maybe your fist or hand holding your head up. Or maybe your hand/fist is near your mouth to catch the words of frustration that you don't want to escape for fear of scaring away the excitement in the room.

The students, undergraduate or graduate, sit with the tempered uncertainty of not knowing whether you agree or not so they pepper their language with "I mean, if you think so and only if you agree, of course." **You nod knowing in your head that they are only doing the proper thing, the thing you've probably taught them when trying to collaborate with someone; make it feel like it was their idea.**

Finally, the question is asked, "So…what do you think?"

You may look at the ceiling. Look out the window. Stare at your screen to help buy time while you try to finesse your thoughts. You put your hands down, clasp them, and you look at your students who look at you as if you could make or break their year with your next words. If you've advised, or have been advised, for a few years – you know this look, you know this feeling, you've been on both sides. Your guard is down and out it comes.

"You know what? Go for it. You can. I won't."

This has been one of my favorite advising tools to help students learn what it takes to put on an event. I've done this whether or not I agree with what they want to do. We, as advisors, can get too invested in the process and don't want our students to fail. We think that sometimes if students fail that means we failed. It doesn't. It means we are doing our jobs.

"You can."

You can go and make those phone calls, just as you were trained and taught.

You can go and write those e-mails, pitch those ideas, and try to get buy-in from campus partners, just as you were trained and taught.

You can run that meeting. Write that copy. Create that draft. Just as you were trained and taught.

You can explore all options and spend time creating a plan A, B, and C to show me that you've thought this completely through. Just as you were trained and taught.

You can lead this team. Envision this process. Follow-through. Just as you were trained and taught.

You can do this. Just as your experience has prepared for this opportunity.

## "I won't."

I won't say you can't. My role is to advise you on all possible scenarios, both in the short and long term.

I won't get upset when you stumble. I've stumbled too, it is how we learn what doesn't work.

I won't tell you can do everything. You can't and you won't, this will take teamwork and support.

I won't relent in my support as you try every possible option. This is an exercise that requires coaching as you try everything you can.

I won't attend every meeting. **I trust that I've shown you the way to ensure that you can do this effectively.**

> *"I trust that I've shown you the way to ensure that you can do this effectively."*

I won't judge your every move. I will process your every move with you so you fully understand the implications, both positive and negative, of your actions. I won't let you regret going through all these processes, procedures, and meetings only to end up with a result you didn't want. **What I will do is show you that everything you've just done, every phone call, e-mail, rejection, successful meeting, and revamping of ideas will make you a good professional in any field.**

"You can. I won't."

This doesn't mean I don't support you. This doesn't mean I'm giving up on you. **This just means I think you are ready to do this on your own and to apply the troubleshooting, creative thinking, and the project & people management skills you've learned from.** If I didn't think so, then I haven't earned the role of being your advisor.

 *As an MBA trained, entrepreneurial minded, and education focused professional, Joe has taken his curiosity to task in efforts to advocate for the reinvention of learning experiences and innovation within education. He is currently the New and First Year Student Experience Specialist at Borough of Manhattan Community College. Some call Joe an instigator while others describe him as an innovator. He considers himself a champion for change. Follow him on Twitter @JoeGinese*

# Advising As Professional Development.

Advising as Professional Development – Tiffany Driver

As the only (full-time) Student Affairs professional at my college of 17,000 students, it's unimaginably easy to lose sight of why I chose Student Affairs in the first place. Every single day, I filter complaints, sign mountains of paperwork, and make strenuous attempts at completing a never-ending to-do list. It can be daunting. **I often times yearn for small remembrances and brief glimpses of why I love working in this profession.**

And then a student enters my office, **"Mrs. Tiffany, it's time for our SGA meeting."** ...and I spend the next hour or two being reminded of just how great Student Affairs actually is.

All things considered, much like professional development, **advising student organizations can revive a tired soul.** At my peak, I advised 10 uniquely different student organizations at one time and I never experienced the SA burnout because the flame was constantly being ignited. In the same manner that professional development tends to give one hope or nurtures the desire to continue work in Student Affairs, so does organization advising.

Higher Education is a vastly changing field, but as professionals that have dedicated themselves to the idea of life-long learning, it is required that we stay connected to the students that we serve (I just learned about Yik Yak a few weeks ago and suddenly it's a very hot SA topic!). Professional development can be more than attending an annual conference, viewing online webinars, and participating in weekly #SAchats; it can also mean taking advantage of the opportunity to formally engage with students outside of the classroom.

While I do value the aforementioned traditional means of professional development, I also value non-traditional professional development: **direct interaction with my students in an organization setting because ultimately—it is what keeps me going.** Traditional professional development can tell us a story or theory about our students; organization advising can allow us the opportunity to see how theory and reality are connected.

**Personally, working in Student Affairs has always been about being fortunate enough to have the opportunity and ability to serve others.** Advising organizations allows me yet another venue to serve students in a greater capacity and oftentimes, outside of my role as a complaint-filtering, signature robot. I don't advise student organizations because it's an expectation of my supervisor or even in my job description because frankly, neither of those actually apply. I advise student organizations because I have a desire to stay connected to the source and subject of the field in which I work.

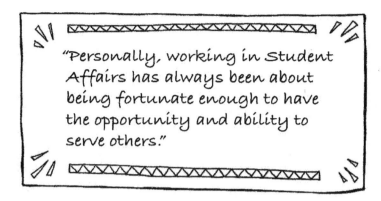

"Personally, working in Student Affairs has always been about being fortunate enough to have the opportunity and ability to serve others."

I use Org Advising to expand my knowledge and experience working with students, increase my current subject area of expertise, and possibly even mature my personal perceptions about the student experience.

**I am intentional about the organizations that I advise.** If I don't support their purpose and their mission, I have no interest in serving as their advisor. However, I will also accept a challenge if I see a gateway to help advance an organization accomplish its goals or refine its mission. Even when I know it may require a little additional work and personal dedication on my end, I'll do it because the investment is worth the return.

Without a doubt, I am a more seasoned professional because I have advised student organizations. **I view Org Advising as a place where I can execute my education and experience but also reshape and transform my practices into proficiencies that effectively and efficiently meet the needs and demands of my students.** Org

Advising balances the mundane tasks (signing paperwork, negotiating with agents, reconciling department expenses) with the rewarding reminder that I chose Student Affairs because I have a desire to make a difference in the lives of students and at the institution in which I work.

*Tiffany Driver, M.Ed is a 10 year #SApro from Katy, Tx. She has worked at both public and private as well as 2 year and 4 year institutions. In her spare time, Tiffany enjoys spending time with husband and family, catching up on her DVR, reading and painting her fingernails. She is also a proud, member of Delta Sigma Theta Sorority, Incorporated. Connect with her on LinkedIn and Twitter @_tiffanyjdriver.*

# Advising for Change

Advising for Change – Kayla Harvey

One of my favorite aspects of my assistantship was co-advising our feminist student organization, FORCE. Like many student organizations, our students worked to put on social justice programming aimed at critically examining how gender is viewed on campus and in society. As advisors, we worked to support their programming and provide general guidance to all of our members. **However, last semester, the role of advising our students began to take on a different shape, as we collectively worked to challenge the status quo.**

One Friday in September, our university's newspaper published a piece on sexual assault that took a strong victim-blaming stance and triggered a few of the students in our group. "We need to do something now," one of members said at our meeting that following Monday. Our students continued to spend parts of their weekly team meetings brainstorming what they could do to get the newspaper to apologize and, since this was not the first problematic piece published, implement training for their staff. My supervisor and I began to sit with our group to plot, plan, and strategically guide our students through the best strategies to meet their desired outcomes. We edited their petitions, coached them through questions to ask and talking points to bring up at their meetings with the leadership of the newspaper. We helped them design a multi-pronged strategy, and we had our own conversations with campus leadership. We worked with our students to try to reach their desired outcomes. In November, the newspaper leadership agreed to implement trainings with their staff the following academic year.

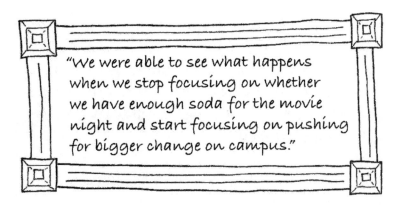

"We were able to see what happens when we stop focusing on whether we have enough soda for the movie night and start focusing on pushing for bigger change on campus."

**We were able to see what happens when we stop focusing on whether we have enough soda for the movie night and start focusing on pushing for bigger change on campus.** It's easy to get bogged down in small details that affect organizations: event contracts, conflict resolution, and whether or not you have the adequate public performance rights to show that particular movie. It's also easy to not try to disrupt problematic actions on our campuses. However, when you're able to step back from the small details and see the bigger picture, you learn the importance of supporting our students in their pain and anger.

 *Kayla is the marketing coordinator for the Office of Admissions at the University of Arizona. Originally from Boston, she graduated with her bachelor's degree in Political Science from Bridgewater State University and will graduate from the University of Arizona with her master's degree in May. In her spare time, Kayla enjoys cooking, reading, and spending time with her partner, Andrew.*

## Mid Level Does Not Mean Middle of the Road – Krista Klein

As a Student Affairs professional approaching five years of advising experience, I find myself at a crossroads. I always question which box to check when asked to identify myself as either an entry level or mid-level professional. I feel like Robert Frost in "The Road Less Traveled", except the checkboxes and self-doubt are the causes of my dilemma. I've spent plenty of time looking down both paths, both reflecting on my experiences since graduate school and looking ahead to my future career goals. **Through this self-reflection, I've made the decision to declare myself a mid-level Student Affairs professional.**

> "Through this self-reflection, I've made the decision to declare myself a mid-level student affairs professional."

How did I come to this conclusion? It's not that one day I woke up and realized that I'm no longer an entry level professional: I've made a long-term commitment to my future in this field, both in and outside of the scope of my job description. My decision to move forward as a mid-level professional, **and more specifically as an advisor**, has been influenced by multiple factors, a few of which I'd like to share with you today: **my advising style and how it's developed over time, my experience handling student activities-related crises, and my ability to prioritize work and life, especially during the time of year we call (gulp) April.**

1. **Developing an advising style:** When I reflect upon my advising experiences and how they've changed from when I began working with student organizations, I think about one of the first large events I oversaw on our campus: a large festival with multiple on-site cooking food vendors (think fire permits and certificates of insurance), inflatables, performances, staging (on muddy grass, of course), and more. This event consumed me for weeks, and it caused me more stress than even some of my most complex professional dilemmas. *This was because I allowed students to define my advising style, rather than me defining it for them.* I welcomed them into my office every time they stopped by unannounced and without an appointment. I nearly tripped over their reimbursement forms and receipts when they slid

them under my door. I called their vendors for them and pleaded for lower prices and faster turnaround times.

2. **When my husband started becoming familiar with the names of my more demanding students after constant venting at the dinner table, I realized things needed to change.** I started telling students that they needed to make an appointment with me before discussing anything related to their organizations. I set up weekly appointments for those who were more demanding or who had more complex events and organizational issues. I drew my advising boundary with a permanent marker, rather than with a pencil. There are still exceptions to the rule, of course, but it has allowed me to put my other work into perspective and realize how many other important issues come across my desk.

3. **Defining and managing crises:** The definition of crisis varies depending on who you ask. For some of my student organizations, a crisis may mean that their chocolate fountain vendor didn't get approved on time, and they won't be able to serve dessert at their date auction. When I receive a pleading e-mail from students to modify my office's policy on contracts with the e-mail subject reading: URGENT, *I take a breath and realize that their*

*definition of crisis is quite different from my own.* Just two years ago, I traveled on an Alternative Winter Break trip to Los Angeles during which my students and I had to evacuate our hotel, and I had to assist a student having a major panic attack in the process. This, to me, is what crisis looks like – and I've been able to manage my stress over many other student-considered "crises" by reflecting upon that experience.

4. **Prioritizing work and life:** I can think of one word that I've eliminated from my advising vocabulary, which has enabled me to grow into a more mature professional: **guilt.** I will no longer allow myself to feel guilty about not attending a student organization event when they've invited me. I can say yes to the events that are most significant to my professional development as an advisor, like attending a large-scale science festival for members of the community, and I can prioritize when my family life is more important than traveling to campus for a student group's fundraising gala. We need to be able to determine when saying yes can benefit us the most, and when it could potentially be harmful to our personal lives.

Since I arrived at that checkbox crossroads, I've come to realize that being a mid-level professional does not mean being "middle of the road." **Becoming a mid-level professional means that we are provided with more opportunities to raise the standard of excellence, to achieve more within and outside the scope of our advising careers, and to face hard Student Affairs challenges head on, even during the chaos swirling around us in April.** How has becoming a mid-level professional impacted your advising style and professional development during the busiest time of year?

*Krista Klein is the Assistant Director for Student Affairs at the Rutgers University Honors College in New Jersey. She is an educator who creates learning experiences for students, more specifically by engaging them with the community and immersing them in community service. Outside of work, she's also a DIY blogger and part-time fitness instructor. Follow along with her at @creatingkrista.*

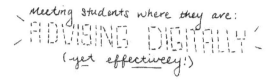

Meeting Students Where They Are: Advising Digitally –
Lindsay Ritenbaugh

If the students with whom you work are anything like mine, they run about a mile a minute. Many students are juggling school, work, and personal lives while doing their best to prepare for their professional futures. **When you add in the responsibilities of being a student leader in (often more than) one student organization, the hours in each day become taken up quickly.** This leaves very little wiggle room in their busy agendas, even if they do share the same amount of time in their day as Beyoncé.

Think about it. **Have you ever tried scheduling a weekly meeting with a group of students?** Trying to find a time that accommodates all advisors and students is easier said than done. Expecting students to find even more free time for advisement in the form of a workshop or training often proves more difficult.

I have found that when students need/want information related to student organization development, it is not always during business hours. Upon returning to the office each morning and having multiple requests for assistance navigating membership in student organizations, processes, and policies, yet seeing little to no attendance at our regularly scheduled student organization workshops, we opted to go in a different direction. **Rather than planning formal workshops where students would receive education and training related to student organization policies, we decided to advise and guide them in a different way – utilizing technology.**

DePaul University uses an online engagement tool for our student organizations. Through this platform, we are able to house the student organization registration process and provide useful resources to students when they need it most (read: when we are likely fast asleep). **By embracing an online venue for student organization support, we are able to accomplish three goals:**

- **increase engagement** between student leaders and our office
- **improve access** to student organization trainings and resources
- provide more efficient student organization **support opportunities**

One example of this is shifting from an in-person workshop model to providing online video tutorials. These videos increase efficiency two-fold: the information is condensed to 6 minutes or less, and it provides an audio and visual representation of the information being presented. Moreover, it can be paused, rewound, or fast-forwarded, and it is available to students whenever they have an immediate need or question. Our office has created several videos to date, including but not limited to:

- Accessing Information about the Student Activity Fee
- How to Apply for Funding through the Student Activity Fee
- How to Create an On-Campus Account for your Student Organization
- How to Create an Event (and Increase Visibility)!
- How to Create a Pre-Registration form for your Event
- How to Request Free Pepsi Products for your Student Organization
- Registering a New Organization
- Renewing Your Student Organization

We continue to seek feedback from students and colleagues about other opportunities to use these video tutorials as part of the educational student organization advising process. [Have one? Email me at lritenba@depaul.edu!]

While we cannot track physical student attendance using this method, we are able to track page views on the YouTube account where these videos are housed. All videos were created [FOR FREE!] through a program called

Screencast-o-matic and are shareable via social media, email, or during an in-person interaction within our office.

## This is not to say that videos are an alternative to advising.

Instead, we have seen more students take advantage of the services and resources our office provides. They spend less time trudging through the snow, catching the train between our two urban campuses, or taking time away from more pressing needs throughout their day. **They work smarter, not harder, to get the information and support necessary to operate effectively as a student organization leader.** Additionally, we are able to better utilize the time spent by the graduate student, undergraduate students, and full-time employees who oversee student organizations. The students we advise are now able to get the "meat and potatoes" necessary for effective student organization operations, both online and at their convenience. Now the time they spend in our physical office locations are saved primarily for one-on-one meetings, executive board meetings, and general student support.

> *"They work smarter, not harder, to get the information and support necessary to operate effectively as a student organization leader."*

How can you incorporate online learning opportunities for the student organizations you advise?

How can you work smarter (rather than harder) with the time you have to spend with your student leaders?

*Lindsay Ritenbaugh oversees 350 student organizations at DePaul University in Chicago, IL. She supervises two undergraduate student involvement ambassadors and one graduate student, while directly advising DePaul's Dance Marathon and Delta Phi Lambda Sorority, Inc. Her free time is spent watching college football (Go Gators!), spending time with Kappa Delta alumnae, playing trivia, and making the most of Broadway in Chicago offerings. Connect with her on social media --> https://about.me/lindsayritenbaugh*

# Student Leaders & mental health.

Student Leaders and Mental Health – Erin Morrell

In my experience, advising student organizations and more specifically, student leaders that are a part of a student organization is a privilege as a Student Affairs professional. There are so many different types of students, with so many backgrounds, and working with them and learning about them and from them is one of the highlights of my job.

**One of the things that I have been spending more and more time with lately are student leaders that also have been dealing with mental illness**, whether it's themselves, a roommate, a close friend or even an immediate family member. Working on a small campus that has some limited resources in terms of professional help for these students, often they come to the staff in Student Affairs to talk, share, and ask for advice. Now, I'm not suggesting that we are mental health counselors in any way, **but we certainly are great resources for our students to be able to let them explain their situation and you, as a Student Affairs professional, can point them in the right direction – whether it's setting them up with the counseling center for an appointment, helping them to find resources off campus that suit their needs, or just advising them to seek help.**

One of the things that I have seen happen more and more over the years is that students tend to come to college with personal issues, concerns, or specific diagnoses that either require regular interaction with counselors, doctors and/or therapists. I have worked with students that have weekly appointments with therapists and have even advised students that have been recommended or required to attend group therapy sessions in order to be successful college students.

Working with these student leaders can be challenging at times, but overall, it makes me better as a Student Affairs professional. We have certainly had to change around meeting times for student organizations that I have advised because a student leader has a standing therapist appointment that we need to work around and I've even had situations occur when a student leader has been admitted to the hospital for a variety of reasons. **These are things that are private issues for the students, and as an advisor, I do everything I can to ensure that the students' privacy is upheld.** For example, if anyone else in the organization questioned why we needed to change the meeting time, I'd simply say that there is a conflict at that time, and we need to agree on another mutually agreeable time. There have been times when one of the student leaders I'm working with has wanted to share their personal situation with the group, but in most cases, they usually want to keep it to themselves. The fact that they recognize that they need help and ask for it is just as important and getting the assistance they need. It also gives other student leaders the chance to be flexible and more accommodating to their fellow student leaders – everyone has their own commitments and sometimes have a special circumstance or reason to change a meeting. **Being part of an organization sometimes means stepping up and helping others when needed.**

I wanted to shed a positive light on working with students that may have mental health concerns **because it doesn't mean that they are incapable of fulfilling their duties or even that they need special accommodations all the time.** Some of these students are the most hard-working and dedicated student leaders that I have worked with, while others sometimes just put unnecessary pressure on themselves to succeed. Sometimes in our field, students with these concerns are stereotyped and stigmatized, whether or not it's on purpose. **It's our responsibility to offer positions to student leaders regardless of their situation and make it work – not only for the student leader, but for their organization and the institution.** College is a time to learn about yourself and giving back to the institution is a great way for students to connect with the institution as a whole.

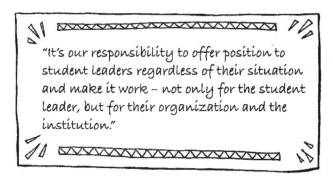

"It's our responsibility to offer position to student leaders regardless of their situation and make it work – not only for the student leader, but for their organization and the institution."

There are times when serious situations may occur, but most of the time, students are just looking for advice and guidance, and overall, the proper resources to help them to be productive and successful student leaders and members of society. Advising student leaders that are members or officers of one or more student organizations on our campus is something that I treasure and really enjoy about my role as an Associate Dean. Being on a very small campus, I still have daily interactions with students and love being a small part of their success as a leader on campus, whether it's today, tomorrow or in the future.

*Erin Morrell is the Associate Dean for Campus Activities and Orientation at Albertus Magnus College (CT). She oversees the Albertus@Night late night programming series, and serves as the director of New Student Orientation. She is an active volunteer with both ACUI and NACA and in her spare time she enjoys traveling, baking and spending time with her friends and family.*

# TWO YEAR HARVEST:
## Advising Student Organizations at a Community College

Two Year Harvest: Advising Student Orgs at a Community College – Kimberly Irland

Advising student organizations at a community college is like **cultivating asparagus**; two years until they are "harvested" by graduation and transfer on, generally speaking. In fact, while gardeners probably wish asparagus would mature faster, I'm jealous they have LONGER (3 years) than I do with most of my students.

I find advising student organizations in a community college setting to be both rewarding and bittersweet. Anyone who advises student organizations knows it takes A LOT of training and time to develop the experiential skills that students need to lead their peers. **We need to cultivate them into leaders**, just like gardeners do with their crops.

I have fond memories as an over-involved student leader in undergrad, a path that ultimately led me to my career in Student Affairs, but I attended a four-year institution. When I started working in campus activities four years ago at a community college, I quickly had to adjust my perspective.

## Five differences struck me right away:

1. Freshman and sophomores were **advancing to leadership roles** typically held by juniors and seniors in four-year settings.

2. Freshman and sophomore leaders **had little to no experience** in their student organizations prior taking on officer roles.

3. Faculty and staff advisors across the college were functioning as **club historians and recruiters** because they were often **one of the only constants from year to year**.

4. To keep clubs truly student-driven, **high turnover in club membership** meant some clubs were not active every semester.

5. With a mostly **commuter population**, student organizations have to compete for student engagement at their meetings and activities during precious college common hours when classes are typically not in session.

So, you can imagine the bitter-sweetness that accompanies advising student organizations in a two-year academic environment with these realities.

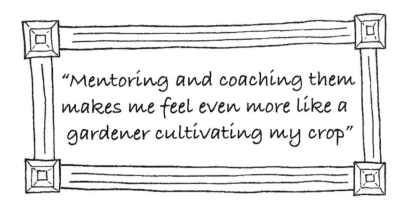

*"Mentoring and coaching them makes me feel even more like a gardener cultivating my crop"*

But my experience at least has been extremely rewarding, too. You see, I'm not just an advisor to these students. I'm their *mentor* and *coach*, and **mentoring and coaching them makes me feel even more like a gardener cultivating my crop**, anxiously awaiting their maturity so I can step back and admire the leaders we graduate. All the hours of training and guiding them as teams and as individuals is contributing to their personal and professional development in ways four-year schools can't match. After all, it's pretty remarkable for them to be able to say, *"I was president of my student organization as a freshman,"* or *"my club gave me officer responsibilities the first semester I joined."* And even though they leave me after two brief years, I know they will go on to do great things in their bachelor's programs, careers and communities. **I'm proud of my harvest.**

 *Kim Irland is the Director of Campus Life at Jamestown Community College. She began her Student Affairs career in Residence Life in 2005, dedicating five years to living on before a brief stint in Student Recruitment and now Campus Life. Kim and her husband live in Jamestown, NY with their two kids and two dogs. Follow her on Twitter @Kimantics.*

*a little risky business*

## A Little Risky Business – Annalise Sinclair

One year ago this May, I accepted my first professional role as the Assistant Director of Student Involvement and Greek Life at a tiny, wonderful college in rural South Carolina. With a solid background in advising and volunteering within fraternity and sorority life, I was fully prepared for every aspect of the "Greek Life" half of my position, **but quickly learned how absolutely clueless I was when it came to the "Student Involvement" piece.** As the advisor for the sole organization responsible for campus activities and programming, I believed that I would have an army of students to help imagine, organize, and implement some of the grand programs I had experienced as an undergraduate student at the tenth largest school in the country. What I was met with was four young ladies who had as much knowledge and experience as I did, and a budget that would cover a quarter of the cost of just one event at my undergraduate institution.

In order to gain some institutional knowledge, I asked the women to walk me through what had been done in the past. According to them, they did the same programs every year, which were calendared for them by their advisor one year in advance. When asked I asked why, I received the same response that I am sure I have heard at least two hundred times since my arrival at the college-"that is the way it has always been done". **This concept of using the word tradition as an excuse to keep doing what is safe and what is comfortable is one that I am all too familiar with from my time advising fraternities and sororities.** We, as Student Affairs professionals, and our students are often terrified to try anything new because the risk of failing is all too real. What if no students show up? What if this is a waste of money during a fiscally challenging year? Or what if our event or organization becomes the laughing stock of Yik Yak?!

> "Two roads diverged in the woods... and I took the road less traveled... AND IT HURT, MAN! Really bad. Rocks, thorns, and glass! My pants broke! Not cool Robert Frost." –Kid President, A Pep Talk from Kid President to You

All it took was one simple question to start a small change that has led to an innovation in campus culture: **What would you do if there were no expectations, no boundaries, or no fear of failure?** Over a four-hour retreat, we created a list of twenty-four potential programs and set our plan for the semester. We threw out the pre-conceived notion of how a programming board should be structured and decided to challenge our student population to try something new, whether that be giant bubble soccer or Hunger Games-style archery with soft-tipped arrows. Admittedly, we experienced some failure, which resulted in the five of us gorging ourselves on candy and watching Grease on a giant blow-up screen... by ourselves. **However, we also experienced great triumph in the form of development and interest in our small organization, growing from four members to fifteen members strong over the course of one semester.**

"What would you do if there were no expectations, no boundaries, or no fear of failure?"

Our journey towards risk taking is culminating in the most controversial break in tradition that the college has yet to experience. For the last thirty years, the end of the spring semester has been celebrated with the Spring Fling concert. Due to the size of our student population and the college's commitment to being fiscally responsible, we are unable to afford the big name artists that many of our neighboring colleges and universities bring in. Last year, we spent several thousand dollars on a concert that only three hundred students attended- an issue attributed to the lack of notoriety of the band and the apathy of a student population bored with "the way we have always done it." At the end of April, the Student Union Board is saying goodbye to "tradition" and bringing in the first Spring Fling Carnival, featuring everything from a Ferris wheel to cotton candy. **Although some students have expressed frustration in the change, the exhilarating feeling of innovation that is slowly creeping across our campus has changed the atmosphere of our school.** We are now seeing other student organizations taking a chance by introducing their own programs and developing new opportunities to for students to interact beyond the classroom. **And it all started with a little risky business.**

*Annalise Sinclair currently serves as the Assistant Director of Student Involvement and Greek Life at Presbyterian College in Clinton, South Carolina. Her role encompasses everything from overseeing fraternity and sorority life to advising the College's programming and activity board. She spends her (limited) spare time as an active Pure Barre enthusiast, fraternity/sorority life advocate, catmom, and proud Presbyterian College Blue Hose.*

## Progress, Not Perfection – Liz Conley

I'm just passing the four-month mark at my current institution, Dean College in Franklin, MA. The past few months have been filled with acclimating, observing, making changes where I can, and growing in excitement for the new beginnings that the fall will bring. One of my main responsibilities is working with all the student-run clubs and organizations.

Within weeks of the students returning from winter break, I realized that the Dean environment is different than my previous institution. Since a large number of our student leaders graduate with an associate degree, we have a higher rate of turnover with club and organization leadership. **This increase in student turnover makes for an interesting environment when considering student-run clubs and their leaders.** In the past, I found emerging sophomore leaders that I could then mold, develop, and grow over their final two years, but Dean's unique climate leaves little time to wait for leaders to emerge. Instead, Dean's environment requires actively engaging the student body to offer students a multitude of opportunities to execute and develop their skills.

After a few weeks of trying to engage clubs and wondering when their large-scale events with educational guest speakers and external vendors would begin, I tried another approach. I started evaluating the current expectations and guidelines for clubs and then began planning adjustments and making plans for the fall. **I realized I was so caught up with making my Dean experience similar to my previous institution, that I wasn't able to appreciate the quirks and unique learning opportunities that Dean was offering me.**

One recent afternoon, after e-mailing another club about its lack of programming and communication with me, I finally realized where I was going wrong. **I was holding clubs to the same standard and wasn't recognizing the differences between each group.** By holding onto my mindset of "how clubs *should* run", I was unable to appreciate the social and educational connections these groups were offering students. Some clubs are an opportunity for students who struggle socially, some are a way to interact with students from other cultures, some provide a support network, and all of them develop life skills for the students.

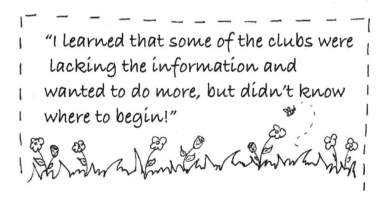

"I learned that some of the clubs were lacking the information and wanted to do more, but didn't know where to begin!"

My objectives were so restricting that I had to let them go and adopt a new mindset of ***"Progress not perfection."*** I typed this mantra and posted it in my office as a daily reminder that small achievements and improvements have an impact as well. I began celebrating small accomplishments and contacting groups more often and the students responded. **I learned that some of the clubs were lacking the information and *wanted* to do more, but didn't know where to begin!** Some groups do not program because it doesn't fit with their club's mission or purpose.

Some time ago, I made the claim that I was a lifelong learner and I'm just now realizing what that entails. **Every institution, department, and student organization responds, learns and functions differently, and it's my privilege to absorb those nuances.** The students at Dean College have taught me to bring my personal mindset into the professional sphere, by accepting people (and student clubs) as they are, meet them where they are, and recognize accomplishments, no matter how small. Because no matter how slow the progress is, it's still progress.

 *Liz Conley was the Campus Center Coordinator during her time at Wheaton College for a one year term position, during which she ignited her passion for working with students. Currently, Liz is at Dean College in Franklin, MA as the Assistant Director of Student Activities & Leadership Development. In her spare time, Liz enjoys going out for breakfast, playing strategic board games, finding new coffee shops and spending lazy rainy days with her fiancé Jack and their cat, CC.*

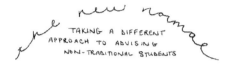

## The New Normal: Taking A Different Approach to Advising Non-Traditional Students – Kristin Staine

Throughout my educational background and Student Affairs internships, I have always been taught what to expect, how to handle a situation, and how to solve any problems that may arise; **what I was not prepared for was advising students who did not feel that they could relate to me.** As a new professional entering into my first post-graduation position, specifically working with student organizations and campus leaders, I took a position at an institution with a large majority of commuter students who fell under that category of "non-traditional." My office was adorned with inspirational quotes and a large collection of souvenirs and memories from my days as a student to help spark a conversation among my newly assigned student organizations. **Yet, I found myself to be working with many students who have had drastically different experiences from myself, and were vocal about believing we couldn't ever successfully work together.**

When I accepted my current position I was still in graduate school and had just turned 24. When I encountered students who had a completely different view on getting involved then I did, I had to alter everything I was told about advising. Within my first year, I worked with one of the student organization's executive board members; she was around my age, balancing school, full-time work, and a two year old. I felt stumped when trying to hold onto a conversation, and quickly altered my approach to include what mattered most to her – her son. **We started with baby steps, literally, by changing our meeting times to accommodate her schedule better, giving permission for her son to attend meetings, and social events.**

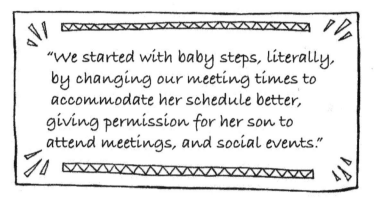

"We started with baby steps, literally, by changing our meeting times to accommodate her schedule better, giving permission for her son to attend meetings, and social events."

This one experience made a huge impact on how I went about advising my student organizations and campus leaders. While this was just one of the experiences I faced while transitioning from a very traditional background to navigating an institution with a unique population of students, I want to be able to assist other professionals who may find themselves in similar situations.

1.  **Age is Just a Number.** All professionals may run into an advising situation where a student may be much younger or a bit older, but it is up to us to change our mindset. The characteristics of non-

traditional students are constantly evolving, so we often need to adjust our views of these students. Do not let your age hinder your advising style, learn how to embrace it! Many students accepted my age and even applauded my quick turn-around into a professional career, but some seemed hesitant to trust me. Utilize your students' life experiences and have them drive the conversation to help keep things neutral.

2. **Think Outside of the Box.** Try to step out of your norm and try to incorporate children and spouses into campus activities to keep students engaged. With our current student population, we have created Family Programming: a department-run initiative that allows students to bring their children with them to enjoy activities in the area without paying out-of-pocket. If you are advising student groups where a few students have children, invest in some stuffed animals to keep in your office. Keeping a plush mascot in your office shows that you care about your students' child, and allows the ideas to keep flowing.

3. **Establish Goals & Expectations.** All students work differently, so make it clear to the students you are advising that you want to help outline their goals and expectations. Help direct your students establish their own road map and get a better sense of why they are there in the first place.

All advisors should feel confident and secure in working with the students they interact with who possess different career and life experiences that differ from their own. **Non-traditional students are becoming the new normal and we need to work to gain a better sense of how they will work better, succeed, and ultimately, accomplish what they came to do.** By expanding our knowledge of what may work better for some of our students, we will better be able to communicate with them and help them succeed.

*Kristin Staine is Assistant Director of Student Activities at Bay State College (MA). She has previously served as a graduate assistant at Boston University and Northeastern University. She holds a bachelor's degree in Communication from Southern New Hampshire University and a master's degree in Higher Education Administration from Northeastern University.*

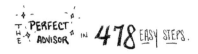

The Perfect Advisor in 478 Easy Steps – Dr. Regina Hyatt

Some of you may remember *The Fish! Philosophy* books and videos featuring the staff of the Pike's Place Fish Market in Seattle. I would always get tickled when watching the video introduction that says the *Fish Philosophy!* would be described in 18 easy steps. I thought I would take it just another step up and describe what the perfect advisor looks like in 478 easy steps! Just kidding! Instead, I think the *Fish! Philosophy* is a great backdrop to some questions and skills that help frame an advising approach that I find very helpful. So here goes...

## Steps 1-119:  Choose Your Attitude

Arguably the most important of the four *FISH!* philosophies, I think it is also the most important of the advising philosophies. While serving as an advisor to a student organization can be exciting and fun, it can also be challenging and time-consuming. The good news is, for the most part, we get to choose which end of this attitude perspective we are going to take. So I choose fun and exciting most every day and even when those challenges crop up (and they certainly will) look for that "Choose Your Attitude" moment to see the situation as absolutely manageable.

## Steps 120-239:  Be There

I like to think of this both in the literal and figurative sense. As an advisor, we sometimes fall into the trap of just signing off on the paperwork. I like to think of our work as more substantive like being there for student events, having meetings with organizational leaders, and generally being aware of their ongoing activities and programs. So be there!

## Steps 240-321:  Make Their Day

I LOVE this! For those of you who are Kouzes' and Posner's Leadership Challenge fans, think of this as Encouraging the Heart. Find those special moments to encourage your student leaders and the work they are doing in their student organizations. One of the things my students like the most are the holiday themed candies that often find their way into their mailboxes in the day or two leading up to a holiday. And here's a helpful hint, if you wait until right after the holiday, you can get boxed candies 50-90% off. Just remember to look at the expiration date (most non-chocolate candy is safe for a year or two).

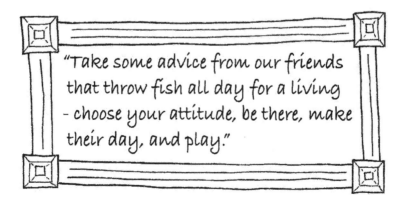

"Take some advice from our friends that throw fish all day for a living - choose your attitude, be there, make their day, and play."

## Steps 322-478:  Play

Every day working with students can be playful and fun. As an advisor, I know how much students appreciate when we take a break from the administrative activities to just have a little bit of fun. Can we say DANCE PARTY? Turning up the music and having a little dance competition is sure to liven up the day. If dancing is not your thing, find another activity that you and your students enjoy. Pull out some crayons, tell a story, or decorate a cupcake. Find something fun to do with your students. Both you and your students will reap the benefits.

Advisors work hard! We know it and so do our students. **Take some advice from our friends that throw fish all day for a living- choose your attitude, be there, make their day, and play.** Follow these 478 easy steps (OK, really just 4) and you are on your way to being an AWESOME advisor!

 *Dr. Regina Young Hyatt is Vice President for Student Affairs at Mississippi State University. Her doctoral work was completed at the University of South Florida in Higher Education Administration. Dr. Hyatt's research interests relate to women in higher education, the impact of student involvement on academic achievement, technology in higher education, and student retention/persistence. Dr. Hyatt's professional involvement included serving as chairperson of the Board of Directors for the National Association for Campus Activities.*

# Advising Isn't Always a DRAG

Advising Isn't Always a DRAG - Meagan Sage

As advisors to student organizations, we often focus on
student development, what we can do to teach and
educate our students, and how we can ensure their
experiences are positive and intentional. Yet we don't
often take the time to reflect on how we learn, develop
and are shaped by the interactions and experiences we
have with the students we advise. I've had a huge number
of powerful, motivational, and educational experiences as
an advisor to many student organizations. When I
reflected on what some of the highlights of those
experiences were, one powerful experience came to mind:
***the time I dressed in drag.***

In April of 2009 I was the Assistant Director of Student
Involvement at Bryant University in Smithfield, RI and was
co-chairing the Student Arts and Speaker Series (SASS), a
committee formed of students, faculty, and staff, whose
goal was to plan more arts and cultural programming on
campus. The group brought many influential and inspiring
speakers to campus, including Elie Wiesel, Common, and
Donna Brazile and planned cultural and arts programs,
including the Young at Heart Chorus, a cake decorating
class, the Capitol Steps political satire chorus and much
more. While the staff and faculty at Bryant worked hard to

create a welcoming culture for all students, it always seemed that environment on campus wasn't as open or supportive for GLBTQ students as it was for others. There weren't a lot of "out" students, which seemed unique for a college campus. At the time, Bryant had a fairly active PRIDE group, but they were small, and besides that there weren't many programs offered to support GLBTQ students or to educate the campus community on GLBTQ issues.

With that in mind, SASS decided to bring the Kinsey Sicks to campus, a group known as "America's Favorite Dragapella Beautyshop Quartet." The quartet, whose four male members dress in drag and perform, are known for their hilarious parodies and songs such as "Macho Man," "Rent a Homo," "Botoxic," "I Will Swallow Him," and more. SASS knew this would be a difficult program to promote, but was confident that it was important to the campus community and brainstormed a list of creative ways to market the program. *This is where my educational moments and life-changing experiences as an advisor came in.* A few of the students on the SASS committee decided that a creative and eye-opening way to promote a drag show was to dress in drag ourselves and go into the dining hall this way to promote the event. The other advisor to SASS, Nick Poche, sat across from me as we watched the students discuss this idea, and some were more comfortable with it than others.

Nick, a great friend and colleague of mine and an out gay man, looked at me and without saying a word, we silently read each other's minds. We told the committee that we wanted to support their idea and that we would dress in drag as well. **While it may seem like no big deal to some, this was a big step for both of us.** Nick had never dressed in drag before, and I certainly hadn't either. Dressing up for a party or an event is one thing, but dressing up to go into the dining hall is quite another. While we knew that it was important to support the students in this way, I'm not sure either of us had any idea how powerful an experience it would be for either of us.

After a few shopping trips and some outfit preparation, the big day finally came. Nick and I got ready together at his on-campus apartment and the students on the committee who had agreed to dress in drag met us. **I can confidently say that I was nervous – the kind of nervous where I get hives and sweat.** What would people think of us? What would they say? How would staff or faculty react to us as administrators on campus dressing in drag? What would I do if students were cruel or hurtful? Although I was nervous, I was also brave, and I walked into the dining hall with the other five committee members dressed in drag, and began promoting our event. My colleagues were supportive, coming to the dining hall to see us and supporting our committee. The students at lunch were fine as well – no one said anything offensive, and no one was rude. Sure, they may have stared or whispered, had questions or been uncomfortable, but we were uncomfortable too and to me, **that is often how learning happens.** After an hour or so, we all changed out of our clothes and went on with our daily routines of meetings, classes, and socializing. We ended up having a great turnout at the Kinsey Sicks show (where Nick dressed in drag again, just for fun) and in the end, we started an important dialogue on Bryant's campus.

"I can confidently say that I was nervous – the kind of nervous where I get hives and sweat."

**Yes, this story is about developing students and teaching valuable lessons, but it is also about the experiences we are given – and can boldly take – as advisors.** I would likely never have dressed in drag if I hadn't been in this situation advising SASS. I wouldn't have known how uncomfortable it can feel to have people stare at you and wonder why you're dressed like "x" when you look like "y." I wouldn't have had the experience of being so nervous to walk into a dining hall because of how I looked that I was sweating and shaking. I wouldn't have felt the pride I felt walking alongside a group of people I knew were doing the right thing at the right time. As advisors, we provide transformational learning experiences for our students, but we are also transformed by the same experiences. The day I dressed in drag, I learned some important lessons, and I role modeled to my students and colleagues that sometimes if you're brave and step outside your comfort zone, you can do amazing things.

*Meagan Sage is the Director of Student Involvement at Southern New Hampshire University, and has worked previously at Johnson & Wales University (RI) and Bryant University (RI). She has been heavily involved with the National Association for Campus Activities since 2001 and is the Chair of the 2015 NACA Northeast Conference.*

"I Want to Do What You Do" - Juhi Bhatt

When I began working at Bergen Community College, BCC, back in the spring of 2011 I was focused on my work as a career and transfer counselor. After all, my internship was based on my master's program for counseling. But as the months went on I began to get a feel and taste for different elements of Student Affairs. Enter student life & student conduct.

In my work as conduct officer I met with students who had an error in judgment and needed assistance in, for lack of better words, righting their wrongs. However, in my work within the office of student life with the student clubs and organizations I was working with the students who were trying to do amazing things at BCC. As an undergraduate student myself I never knew an office such as this existed. An office that plans events? An office that oversees 50+ clubs? **The office of student life opened my eyes to the possibilities that awaited me as a Student Affairs professional.**

It was due to my work in this office that I began to work with the Student Government Association (SGA). At first I was like a consultant. Someone that the senators and executive board could come to see if they ever had questions about career/transfer counseling. But as time went on, I was asked to be a co-advisor to the organization. **It is within this past year that I have truly seen what that role can do for my students.**

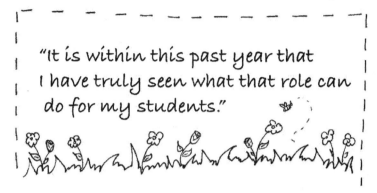

"It is within this past year that I have truly seen what that role can do for my students."

Enter my student government vice president of this year. The moment I met this young lady I knew she was going to do amazing things. She has and will continue to have a fire within her that most do not have that most do not use to their advantage. And although it may seem she knew that she wanted to be a part of the student government association from the very beginning, she did not. She became the vice president by happenstance.

When I first met, we will call her Natalie for privacy purposes, back in the fall of 2013, she had no idea what organization she wanted to be a member of at BCC. She came to me under the recommendation of my then supervisor who asked me to meet with her as a counselor to help her narrow down what she wanted to be involved in at BCC. **Natalie had decided she was going to be a senator, an executive board member for LASA, our Latin** student organization, SAB, our student activities board, all while maintaining her 4.0 and 12 credits at BCC. Now mind you she was already working practically full time as well.

It was for the aforementioned reasons that I recommended that Natalie find the one thing that made sense for her in order to give back to BCC. As the year progressed Natalie began to weed out the organizations that did not feel were right for her and when spring 2014 approached she had decided she would be a senator for the upcoming year. I knew that she would make a great senator but an even better executive board member. I asked Natalie if she had thought about running for a position within the executive board **and she said no because she had never been a senator. I replied with, "So what?"**

We left that meeting with an undecided answer, but by the end of the week Natalie had decided she was going to run for chief of staff. However, fate had other plans for her. Although Natalie won her position of chief of staff in the fall of 2014 she had to step up and fill the role of vice president. It is within this role that Natalie has been exposed to the field of Student Affairs in her work with the SGA and our office.

She enjoys reading policies at the institution and being a student advocate while navigating the politics and organizational culture at BCC. It is for these same reasons that she has decided to pursue a career in Student Affairs. **I will never forget the day she came into my office and said, "Juhi, I want to do what you do."** And so this upcoming June I will be bringing Natalie with me to the NASPA Region II conference in DC so that I can begin paying it forward to her as many in the field have done with me.

As an SGA advisor, I have seen first-hand the benefits of students who take part in the holistic collegiate experience. Students who work within clubs on campus are exposed to things such as programming, budget, policy and processes that can assist in their development as leaders and students. **The end product is a student who is ready to transfer those skills to his or her next institution or his or her career.** After all, aren't transferrable skills what our field is all about?

In the years to come I look forward to seeing this young lady take over the field of Student Affairs. I hope to be at her most important moments in order to celebrate with her. And I hope she pays it forward with her future student leaders within the clubs and organizations she works with, at whatever school she lands. **Ultimately, the best way to see the success of your work is in your students.**

 *Juhi Bhatt is currently the Coordinator of Judicial Affairs & Student Information at Bergen Community College. Along with being the conduct officer at the institution Juhi serves as the case manager for the Behavioral Intervention Team (BIT), supervisor of the student information desk and as co-advisor to the Student Government Association. Within the Office of Student Life & Student Conduct, Juhi assists with the planning and implementation of new student orientation and commencement. Follow Juhi on twitter @jbhatt12*

When the Noise Keeps Me From Listening - Jason Meier

I'm a tech nerd. I've got dual screens on my desktop, an iPad always nearby, and my Galaxy Note 3 is normally on my desk. To make this perfectly clear, on a normal day there are four digital devices lit up on my desk. And if a device is on, there's probably a social media app open.

It's not just Facebook. I've got Twitter and Tweetdeck, Google Hangouts, Skype, and Snapchat blazing across my screens. Between those, and the constant email barrage (mostly spam, I'm not that important), **my computer and iPad, and phone never stop making noises.**

**I'm constantly distracted by things flashing in front of me.** You're probably distracted, too. You just haven't really thought about it.

Play a little game with me – turn the volume up on your computer, tablet, and phone and turn on the notifications. Do you hear those pings and beeps and whirrs? Let them go full blast for a few hours while you try to work with students. No, really. Do it. I'll wait for you.

Great. Now that you've turned everything on, **try to hold a meaningful one-on-one conversation when your phone**

**won't stop vibrating.** Try to listen to a student share their agenda for an upcoming meeting when you're busy waiting for an important email. Try to focus during a student organization meeting when your laptop won't stop beeping at you. **Just try to effectively advise an organization's executive board when you're surrounded by all of this noise.**

> "Just try to effectively advise an organization's executive board when you're surrounded by all of this noise."

It's hard. We're so constantly distracted that **we've stopped fully listening to things going on around us**, even when they're going on in our own offices.

This problem sneaks up on you. You may have not noticed yet, but your students have probably noticed it. **We've become too busy anticipating an interaction that we're missing the everyday interactions with our own students.**

How are we advising our students when there is so much noise coming from so many directions? Access to technology and social media have done amazing things for our profession, **but it has also turned us into terrible listeners.**

In one-on-one advising meetings, are you turning your screen off, putting your tablet away, and turning your phone to silent? How can you hear your student over all of the noise? How can you advise when it's so loud?

I realize I'm doing a bad job of this, but I want to do better and I want to do better with you.

So I challenge you to do a few things this week:

- ☐ The next time you have a one-on-one meeting with a student leader, have a conversation with the student about what it means to listen.
- ☐ Turn off your phone.
- ☐ Logout of Facebook, Twitter and Instagram.
- ☐ Close your Outlook or Gmail.
- ☐ Or, leave it all in your office and have a meeting with a student outside, in a place with fewer tech-related distractions.

Give it a try. Let me know how it goes. I promise I'll disconnect from everything and listen to you.

 *Jason Meier is doing his best to disconnect and listen to the students of Emerson College right now. Located in Boston, Emerson College devotes itself to the study of communication, while bringing innovation to communication and the arts. In his spare time, you can find Jason awkwardly dancing at a concert, exploring the local food scene or hanging out with his cat, Lil' Poundcake. Continue the conversation with Jason on Twitter at @jasonrobert.*

LGBTQA
STUDENT ORGANIZATIONS
AT RURAL SCHOOLS

## LGBTQA Student Organizations at Rural Schools - Nathan Meints

For my entire professional career I have had the opportunity and privilege to work at higher education institutions in rural areas. Being born and raised in rural areas I find these sparsely populated regions to be my home.

However, to some, my chosen rural residences sometimes flies contrary to my queer identity. People will ask why gay people would *want* to live in a rural area. LGBTQA culture is seen and represented from a lens of a "big city". The US Department of Agriculture has found that about 10% of same-sex couples live in rural areas. **Despite this fact, it is often assumed that LGBTQ people are only found in large communities.**

The perception that queer issues are an urban concept trickles down to the work I do while working with queer students and advising LGBTQA student organizations. Over the past few years I have been able to research queer student identity development in rural areas. **Advising student organizations in rural schools can be incredibly difficult.** As a case study, please consider the following: most college and universities today have at least one student organization for LGBTQA students. However, many non-rural and larger schools will commonly have more than one. Why is this important? Typically, the more LGBTQA organizations that exist at a school, the more diverse their focus.

This becomes increasingly difficult when considering the diverse amount of students we serve. For example, the group I currently advise is the only LGBTQA affiliated group on campus. **We must somehow (as a single organization) serve students that want to belong to a purely social organization and those that want to pursue advocacy against homophobia and heterosexism.** At one point in time, a non-traditionally aged student came to a meeting. The meeting was largely made up of first-year students that came to the meetings as a safe-place social venue. However, the non-traditional student wanted the organization to organize protests and other advocacy issues. The group did not share this view. The non-traditional student never came back to a meeting – their needs were not met. At a larger school or at a school with more LGBTQA organizations, this student could of found a better fit in an organization. Instead, this student never came to a group meeting again.

**This non-traditional student could very well represent a variety of identities.** It could be a student of color not feeling comfortable in a largely white organization. It could be a trans* student not feeling like their needs are not being discussed, or even recognized. Simply put, when at a rural school with only one LGBTQA organization, it is often seen as a "catch all" organization for all LGBTQA peoples.

How do we address this problem? The easy answer would appear to "simply" create more organizations. **However, if you work at a small rural school, you know that many times resources are limited.**

I don't think there is an easy answer. I think the uneasy answer is a community based journey of advocating for LGBTQA students. Whether or not you personally advise a LGBTQA student organization, I ask you as a Student Affairs professional to advocate for both individual LGBTQA students and their organizations. This can come in many forms: attending programs, allocating funds, and offering assistance. Change often comes slow in rural areas. **It truly takes a community effort to support, embrace, and educate a new generation of students.**

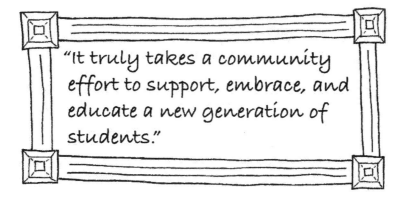

"It truly takes a community effort to support, embrace, and educate a new generation of students."

My purpose in writing a piece on rural LGBTQA student organization advising is to give hope to others. **It is hard to work with organizations that are under-recognized and over-burdened.** Please know that the work we do in rural areas is not only important, but essential. Even though we don't have all the tools readily available that our students ask for, I truly believe that students in rural areas can feel the passion of the work we do. Regardless of if a LGBTQA student is from an urban area or a rural area it is our responsibility as Student Affairs practitioners to support students the best we can with the resources we have.

*Nathan is a hall director at Bemidji State University. His professional interests include LGBTQA student development theory and applying classical sociological theory to student development theory. Follow him on twitter @nmeints.*

Resources

## Introducing Our Series on Advising Student Organizations
- http://www.nacada.ksu.edu/Resources/Clearingho use/View-Articles/Advising-as-teaching-resource-links.aspx

## Navigating the Revolving Door of Club Leadership
- Miller, M. T., Pope, M. L., & Steinmann, T. D. (2005). A profile of contemporary community college involvement, technology use, and reliance and selected college life skills. College Student Journal, 39(3), 596–603.
- National Center for Education Statistics. (2010). Digest of Education Statistics (No. NCES Publication No. 2011-015). U.S. Department of Education. Retrieved from http://nces.ed.gov/pubs2011/2011015.pdf
- Orozco, V., & Cauthen, N. K. (2009). Work less, study more & succeed: How financial supports can improve postsecondary success. New York, NY: Demos. Retrieved from http://www.careerladdersproject.org/docs/st udymore_web.pdf

## Advising for Change
- https://www.facebook.com/ASUA.FORCE

**Meeting Students Where They Are: Advising Digitally (yet Effectively)**

- https://orgsync.com/29891/videos/29161
- https://orgsync.com/29891/videos/29162
- https://orgsync.com/29891/videos/30207
- https://orgsync.com/29891/videos/30764
- https://orgsync.com/29891/videos/29972
- https://orgsync.com/29891/videos/30317
- https://orgsync.com/29891/videos/31593
- https://orgsync.com/29891/videos/31605
- http://www.screencast-o-matic.com/

# BONUS: Audio Recordings

As if the content in this book isn't enough, we wanted to give you something a little extra special by having each contributor record an audio version of their post. This is a free gift from all of us to you, as a way of saying "Thanks!" for continuing to support The Student Affairs Collective. You can find, and download, an MP3 of each contributor here > https://goo.gl/PH8Mps and use the password "BeyondMeetings"

# Here's To Your Continued Success!

*a* Student Affairs Collective book

Made in the USA
Lexington, KY
16 August 2016